proclamation 2

Aids for Interpreting the Lessons of the Church Year

lent

Marianne H. Micks and Thomas E. Ridenhour

series c

editors: Elizabeth Achtemeier · Gerhard Krodel · Charles P. Price

FORTRESS PRESS PHILADELPHIA

Second printing 1982

Library of Congress Cataloging in Publication Data (Revised)

Main entry under title:

Proclamation 2.

Consists of 24 volumes in 3 series designated A, B, and C which correspond to the cycles of the three year lectionary plus 4 volumes covering the lesser festivals. Each series contains 8 basic volumes with the following titles: Advent-Christmas, Epiphany, Lent, Holy Week, Easter, Pentecost 1, Pentecost 2, and Pentecost 3.

CONTENTS: [etc.]—Series C: [1] Fuller, R. H. Advent-Christmas. [2] Pervo, R. I. and Carl III, W. J. Epiphany.—Thulin, R. L. et al. The lesser festivals. 4 v.

1. Bible—Homiletical use. 2. Bible—Liturgical lessons, English.

[BS534.5.P76] 251 79-7377

ISBN 0-8006-4079-9 (ser. C, v. 1)

269J82 Printed in the United States of America 1-4082

Contents

Editor's Foreword

Lent is an ancient observance. A two-day fast in preparation for Easter was already observed early in the third century; and the rest of Holy Week was included at an only slightly later date. The extension of the Lenten season to the previous five weeks represented by this volume is implied by a passing reference to the "forty days" in one of the canons of the Council of Nicaea in 325. No details are given there. One assumes that the reference is to a custom already well established. From descriptions later in the fourth century we learn that the "forty days" were a period of deepened preparation for candidates to be baptized on Easter Eve. Inevitably this forty-day fast came to be associated with Jesus' fasting and temptation in the wilderness mentioned by Matthew, Mark, and Luke. The reading of the temptation story as the liturgical Gospel on the First Sunday in Lent is a venerable Western tradition.

As the observance of Lent has developed, the whole church seeks year after year to approach the crucifixion and resurrection of the Lord with the same intensity and freshness as the newest candidates for baptism did at the beginning. In the cycle of readings covered in this volume, the Gospel readings treat our Lord's life and teachings through representative passages in the Gospel according to Luke, from the temptation story to the ominous parable of the wicked tenants. The Old Testament lessons, on the other hand, assist us to make this approach by their rehearsal of God's saving acts on behalf of Israel. Epistles comment on these other lessons in the light of new life in Christ.

We offer the present volume in the hope that it will aid preachers of the Word to engage their congregations more effectively in their approach to the paschal mystery. The exegetical treatment of each appointed lesson addresses the question, What did it mean in its own time? Yet the preacher cannot stop with the answer to this question. In fact, his work has scarcely begun. Like medieval painters who depicted biblical stories in medieval European settings and dressed biblical characters in medieval clothes, a preacher must do a major work of translation. He must make the old story appear in contemporary dress so that his hearers can more readily identify themselves with it and can place themselves more intelligently within the range of the gospel message. The homiletical material of this volume, therefore, is directed to the second question which a preacher must answer: What can the passage mean to us now? No answer to either the first question or the second is set in concrete. That is why this is a volume of *aids*. Finally preachers must answer both questions for themselves. Nevertheless, significant answers to these two questions will be of major assistance in the preacher's task.

The exegetical portion of this volume has been prepared by Marianne H. Micks, Professor of Biblical and Historical Theology at the Protestant Episcopal Theological Seminary in Virginia at Alexandria. She is the author of *Introduction to Theology* and *The Future Present*, in addition to various articles and reviews in *Anglican Theological Review* and *The Journal of Religion.*

The homiletical sections were written by Thomas E. Ridenhour, Assistant Professor of Homiletics at Lutheran Theological Seminary in Gettysburg, Pennsylvania. He has contributed articles and reviews to *The Bulletin* and *Dialog*, publications of the Lutheran Church.

Alexandria, Va. CHARLES P. PRICE

Ash Wednesday

Lutheran	Roman Catholic	Episcopal	Pres/UCC/Chr	Meth/COCU
Joel 2:12-19	Joel 2:12-18	Joel 2:1-2, 12-17 or Isa. 58:1-12	Zech. 7:4-10	Zech. 7:4-10
2 Cor. 5:20b—6:2	2 Cor. 5:20—6:2	2 Cor. 5:20b—6:10	1 Cor. 9:19-27	1 Cor. 9:19-27
Matt. 6:1-6, 16-21	Matt. 6:1-6, 16-18	Matt. 6:1-6, 16-21	Luke 5:29-35	Luke 5:29-35

EXEGESIS

First Lesson: Joel 2:12-19. Appropriate as it is for Ash Wednesday, this section of the book of the prophet Joel presents a number of problems for the exegete. There is little or no consensus as to when or why the citizens of Jerusalem were summoned to a solemn assembly. The book provides little internal evidence for dating, although the weight of current scholarship leans toward the early postexilic period—roughly ca. 500–400 B.C. Similarly, debate continues as to whether the plague of locusts which brought about the devastating famine described in the first chapter was a genuine historical event or a metaphorical way of picturing the advancing Day of the Lord. Internal detail such as those perplexed cattle who cannot find pasture (1:18) seems to favor the former judgment.

If this be true, then the priests and cultic prophets of Israel are calling the citizens together in a time of national crisis. They are convinced that "yet even now" (v. 12) a return to the Lord can avert further disaster. The summons to national mourning and sincere repentance is answered, according to the reading, quite concretely. "Behold," says the Lord, "I am sending to you grain, wine, and oil" (v. 19). The whole passage rests on the profound conviction that what is done in worship affects not just the individual believer but the whole fabric of society.

Covenant motifs are present from the outset. "Return to me" (v. 12) presupposes that straying away from intimate relationship with God which the prophets of Israel universally condemn. The call to "rend your hearts" stresses the necessity of opening up the whole self toward God. The thought is close to that of Jer. 24:7: "I will give them a heart to know that I am the Lord: and they shall be my people and I will be their God, for they shall return to me with their whole heart." The Joel verse is not making any negative judgment on the value of external actions, however; it enjoins fasting and weeping, traditional manifestations of repentance.

The character of the God of Israel is reviewed in traditional prophetic language in v. 13. Dominant are the notes of his grace and mercy and love—a fact which should be underlined for those modern Marcionites who depict the God of the OT as primarily a God of wrath. V. 14 boldly envisions God himself visiting his people at worship and leaving behind him the very materials for offering, grain and wine, which are now virtually unavailable in the land afflicted by drought (cf. 1:9).

Given that faith-picture of what a national fast might accomplish, the prophet calls for the shofars to sound in Jerusalem (v. 15) and for people of all ages and all conditions of life to come together. Men, women, and children are here explicitly all essential members of the people of Israel (v. 16).

The priests are positioned in the traditional place of prayer in the temple, between the porch and the altar (v. 17; cf. Ezek. 8:16), to lead intercessions. Here, as indeed throughout the passage, the tone is that of a corporate lament such as Psalm 74, with its appeal to God to arise and plead his cause because the impious are scoffing at him.

Notable in the concluding verses is the interconnection between the reputation of Yahweh and that of the people of Israel. The people ask him to vindicate himself. Why should the other nations say, "Where is their God?" (v. 17). He answers, "I will no longer make you a reproach among the nations" (v. 19). The well-being of Israel is uppermost in the mind of the Lord, according to this prophetic oracle. He is responsive to their needs, even to the point of considering their international reputation.

Second Lesson: 2 Cor. 5:20—6:2. St. Paul is talking in this portion of his Second Letter to the Corinthians about both the ministry and the message of reconciliation which he has just declared (5:18–19) that God has given to him and his fellow workers. V. 20 summarizes both his ministerial authority and the content of the good news he preaches. The theological basis of that message is then boldly set forth in a single-sentence paradox (v. 21). The reading closes with what is essentially a rephrasing of what he has just said, buttressed by scriptural quotation and commentary (6:1–2). As is so often the case, the chapter division was inappropriate at this point; the lectionary rightly recognizes the continuity of thought.

Ambassadors in the Roman Empire were understood to be the personal representatives of the emperor himself. When Paul claims to be speaking for Christ (in behalf of), he is claiming a very high degree of authority for his apostleship. Yet as he had shortly before made clear in this letter (4:5; 5:12), he is not boasting about his own position. Rather, he is explaining his commission to carry on the very servanthood of Christ. When he speaks in that role, God speaks through him.

The appeal, which has the force of imploring, even begging, is to be reconciled to God. There is no *you* in the Greek text, so the effect is more that of a universal exhortation than of a direct charge to the Corinthian Christians. To be reconciled to God means to appropriate his offer, to allow him to overcome any enmity between ourselves and God, to recognize that no grounds for alienation remain. Paul may be drawing on earlier Christian tradition in his use of the language of reconciliation in this chapter. In any case, he makes it emphatic that God has taken the initiative and opened for us the possibility of a new relationship of peace with and closeness to himself.

V. 21 states the grounds for this new possibility almost in poetic form. The sentence should not be read as support for any specific later doctrine of the atonement, nor watered down in the interests of logic. As in the comparable statement of Gal. 3:13, "having been made a curse for us," the emphasis is on "for our sake." Whether or not Paul is consciously alluding to Isa. 53:5, he is certainly affirming the completeness of Christ's identification with the sinful human condition. At the same time he affirms the fact that Christ "knew no sin." There are no grounds for referring this phrase to the preexistent Logos rather than to the earthly Jesus in order to dissolve the mystery.

Christ's full identification with humanity was in order that we might become not righteous, be it noted, but participant in God's own righteousness. The phrase "in him" ends the sentence in the Greek and deserves special attention. The righteousness of God is in Christ.

In 6:1 the translators have supplied "with him" to qualify Paul's idea of working together, but that sense is implicit from the preceding sentences. As God's co-worker, Paul implores the Christians to let the grace of God really make a change in their lives. He quotes Isa. 49:8 from the Septuagint to underline the fact that they are living in a time of favor, in a day when God has helped them. Therefore he can twice repeat the jubilant "behold" of his commentary on the prophet's eschatological vision, and twice stress the graceful "now." Contrary to the popular notion that Paul is speaking in a threatening tone, telling his readers to shape up because tomorrow may be too late, he is positively rejoicing in the possibilities of the present age. The "day of salvation" has begun.

Gospel: Matt. 6:1-6, 16-21. The Sermon on the Mount as we have it shows similarities to a handbook of church discipline for use by the church of Matthew's day. The material here, along with that of the other discourses in this Gospel, has been shaped for Jewish-Christian teaching purposes, probably in conscious contrast to the reshaping of Pharisaic tradition under way at Jamnia in the same period. This means that the sermon is addressed to the needs of the church of the postwar world, following the destruction of Jerusalem in A.D. 70.

The section from chap. 6 appointed for today presupposes Christian continuation of the traditional Jewish triad of religious duties—almsgiving, prayer, and fasting. Throughout the chapter the importance of inner motivation is set forth over against mere ostentation and public display of piety. Nevertheless similar demands for sincerity and integrity in worship can be found in rabbinic writings of the same era. Jewish as well as Christian leaders have long been aware of the dangers of hypocrisy, or mere playacting, which so easily trip up religious people.

In 6:1 two major themes are introduced. First, Christians are to avoid performing their religious duties in order that other people may be impressed. Three times in what follows Jesus uses the same formula to pronounce judgment on such motivation: "Truly, I say to you, they have their reward" (vv. 2, 5, 16). If you seek and get human praise for being pious, you have already been paid in full. The word translated "reward" is a commercial term such as would be stamped on a paid-up account.

Second, however, when people rightly hunger and thirst after righteousness, they are rewarded by the Father in heaven. In the context of the sermon the idea of reward is to be understood in the light of the Beatitudes. The same word translated "righteousness" in 5:6 is translated "piety" in 6:1, and the notion of reward is introduced (without apology) first in 5:12.

Alms are to be given without public noise (v. 2). The clause about not letting your left hand know what your right hand is doing is a striking metaphor; we are impoverished when it is paraphrased, "do it in such a way that even your closest friend will not know about it" (TEV). Bonhoeffer was closer to the meaning when he said that we should hide our righteousness even from ourselves, that the verse is talking about love in the sense of spontaneous, unreflective action.

Prayer is likewise not an activity for the purpose of public show. In spite of the charge to go to your room and shut the door (v. 6), an allusion to Isa. 26:20, this cannot be taken as a prohibition of corporate worship. Jesus' own practice contradicts such a privatistic view of prayer, as well as the plural pronouns of the Lord's Prayer which follows in Matt. 6:9–13. Matthew uses hyperbole to get his point across.

Fasting was already an accepted part of Christian piety in the primitive church, in spite of the Gospel reports that Jesus himself was criticized for not fasting (cf. Matt. 9:14–15; 11:18–19). The Didache 8:1 instructs Christians to fast on Wednesdays and Fridays in order to be distinguished from the Jews, who fast on Mondays and Thursdays. Once again the concern here is with the inner motivation for this or any other spiritual discipline.

The sayings which conclude this section (vv. 19–21) underline this understanding of what has just been said. They appear in Luke in another context (12:33–34). Put here they reinforce the contrast between a well-advertised human reputation for piety—which can evaporate overnight—and a sound and silent investment in heaven. In v. 21, as distinct from vv. 19–20, the "treasure" is singular and the second person singular is used. This is probably a saying which circulated independently, therefore. Put here it echoes the relatively unusual use of the second person singular in 6:4, 6, and 18—"*thy* Father." An intimate, personal relationship with God appears to be the treasure or reward envisioned throughout.

HOMILETICAL INTERPRETATION

Ash Wednesday is the liturgical doorway through which the church enters on its Lenten path of preparation for the Easter feast. The path leads to Golgotha and the garden where God acted in Jesus to win his cosmic victory over Satan, sin, and death. The shadow of the tree and the light from the empty grave permeate the church's Lenten journey. All of the texts assigned for the Lenten season need constantly to be read and studied and preached under the shadow of the cross and the light of the resurrection. The death and resurrection of Jesus are the central content of the church's proclamation in this time of preparation. It is God's act in Christ that makes possible the church's preparation for the feasting of Easter.

Lenten preparation revolves around three actions of the preacher and his hearers. The first action is that of *reflection.* The Lenten journey is a time for reflection upon the activity of God in his world and in the life of his people. This reflection is based not only upon the Scriptures as the witness to this divine work but also upon contemporary events which testify to God's presence and action in our own day and life. We recall and proclaim all these mighty acts of God so that our people may perceive them too.

A second action in our preparation for Easter is that of *introspection.* Introspection is a serious look at ourselves and our community of faith in light of God's passion for us and with us, as well as our passion for our neighbors and our world. This action is not navel gazing but an honest and deep look at who we are and what we are, as God has made us and as he wants us to be.

Finally, there is the *perception* that arises out of the reflection and introspection. This perception centers on the new possibilities and responsibilities that God gives to his people and sets before them as he continues to be present in their lives to forgive and free them. A new perception can often surprise and enliven God's people, which is the heart of the good news of God's victory for us and his world.

On the day when we begin our annual Lenten journey to the cross, the church is met by the cry of the lessons to begin preparation. To prepare involves specific action in all three texts. In Joel the cry is to repent—"Rend your hearts and not your garments." In Paul's letter to Corinth, the cry is, "on behalf of Christ, be reconciled to God." The gospel's call is for the hidden, unobtrusive practice of piety in almsgiving, prayer, and fasting.

However, the action to which the church is called is not the primary focus. Each of the assigned texts proclaims that God has already acted, and this action of God motivates and enables our preparation during Lent (see Joel 2:13; 2 Cor. 5:21).

First Lesson: Joel 2:12–19. The short Book of Joel could profitably be read by the preacher to place this text into its larger context. The locust plague (Is it real or symbolic? See exegesis.) is described with realistic images and is stated to be the judgment of God upon his people. The prophet calls upon God's people to repent, to turn the whole self to God, and perhaps the calamity may be averted.

What is the basis of this call to repentance? Is it the action of the people that will cause God to change his mind? Will the rending of hearts and not garments move God to take away the judgment? Not from the prophet's perspective. This will not be the sequence of events. Just the reverse. The call to repentance is rooted in God's prior action to and for his people. God is gracious and merciful. Uppermost in the mind of God is the well-being of his people. The very fact that God sends the prophet to call the people to repentance evidences God's care and concern.

For the contemporary church, what are the evidences of God's continued care for his people? Where are the actions of God that manifest his concern for the well-being of his people today? These gracious acts of God today are the basis for the contemporary call of God to his people to turn to God in repentance.

The call to repentance in the text is a call to the community of Israel. It involves both the individual person in Israel and the nation as a whole. Repentance is generally called for in individual ways in our world today. Preachers must ask what the sins are from which their congregation is called to turn. What are the rebellions against God, and the pains inflicted upon the neighbors, from which God calls his people to turn away and thus return to him?

Repentance is rooted in God's gracious love and care for his people. It is God's action in the death and resurrection of Jesus that establishes the relationship of trust and obedience between God and his people. Out of this relationship God calls his people continually to repentance. As Frederick Buechner writes, "To repent is to come to your senses. It is not so much something you do as something that happens. True repentance spends less time looking at the past and saying, 'I'm sorry,' than to the future and saying 'Wow!'" (*Wishful Thinking—A Theological ABC* [New York: Harper and Row, Publishers, 1973], p. 79).

Second Lesson: 2 Cor. 5:20—6:2. There are two major concerns in this text. The primary concern is the good news that God has acted in Jesus to overcome all of the rebellion and sin that human beings have done to alienate themselves from the One who loves them continually. The act of reconciliation by God was a radical and costly one. He made Jesus, who "knew no sin," to become sin—to enter our sinful and estranged world—in order that the broken relationship might be healed. Paul appeals to the Corinthians—and to all people—to allow God to overcome any alienation that remains, for in reality there are no grounds left for enmity between God and his people.

The cross is at the center of Paul's word of reconciliation. Through this lesson, its shadow hangs over the beginning of the Lenten journey. One asks, Where are the realities of the cross's action of reconciliation in our contemporary world? The healing that does occur in broken family relationships can reflect the agony and the power of God's reconciling power. The sacraments of baptism and the Lord's Supper also offer images and realities of God's reconciling action touching the lives of people today.

There is a second important word in this text. Paul speaks of being Christ's ambassador and of God's making his appeal through him. The reconciliation God works in the lives of his people sets a task before them. We become God's ambassadors in our world. How well do we, in our local congregations and communities, fulfill this task that God gives to us? How well do we become the channels through which God's appeal is made to the world? What is the nature of this task in the situation in which you and your congregation find yourselves? The task can be done because God has reconciled us to himself in Christ.

The note of urgency for this task is sounded also. "Behold, now is the acceptable time; behold, now is the day of salvation" is not a threat (see the exegesis) but is rather a God-given opportunity and possibility to become what God has already made his people: reconciled men and women who are Christ's ambassadors for the world.

Gospel: Matt. 6:1-6, 16-21. The very real danger when preaching on a text from the Sermon on the Mount is to turn it into a new and heavy demand. The exegesis shows that the text refers to the Beatitudes (Matt. 5:1–12). This word about the conduct of life in the kingdom of God is spoken to those persons who "hunger and thirst after righteousness," whom God has already blessed. The action portrayed and described in this text is the follow-through of the life of faith. The very one who speaks these words about the living of the Christian life is the one who gave his life to make the new life possible for his people.

During the Lenten journey, religious practices and actions become more numerous in the preparation for Easter. The text speaks of acts of almsgiving, prayer, and fasting. Historically the church has held these actions to be helpful and good discipline for the faithful. But why are they to be done? What is the motivation for such actions? The text says very clearly that such acts of piety are not to be done for ostentation and public show. These acts of the new life are done silently, hiddenly, because they spring from an inner motivation. They need no praise nor human glory. The inner motivation arises from the new heart—the new life—that has been given in being blessed by God in Christ Jesus.

The Lenten journey of preparation for Easter feasting can helpfully discipline and strengthen the life of the Christian and the church. What are the acts of piety—of almsgiving, prayer, and fasting—that are appropriate and needed by your congregation? What are the acts of piety that can be of caring love and service for the people in your community? The new perception that can arise from the reflection and introspection in dealing with this text can helpfully open new vistas of Lenten and Christian discipline for the people of God in today's world.

The First Sunday in Lent

Lutheran	Roman Catholic	Episcopal	Pres/UCC/Chr	Meth/COCU
Deut. 26:5-10	Deut. 26:4-10	Deut. 26:(1-4) 5-11	Deut. 26:5-11	Deut. 26:1-11
Rom. 10:8b-13	Rom. 10:8-13	Rom. 10:(5-8a) 8b-13	Rom. 10:8-13	Rom. 10:5-13
Luke 4:1-13	Luke 4:1-13	Luke 4:1-13	Luke 4:1-13	Luke 4:1-13

EXEGESIS

First Lesson: Deut. 26:5-11. All of the OT lessons for Lent (Series C) deal with God's great actions in history on behalf of his people Israel. They set before us the basic motifs in biblical understanding of the nature of God and of his concern for human affairs, both public and private. Following today's summary of the mighty events which were decisive for Israel's faith (and for that of the new Israel), we are presented on subsequent Sundays with God's special self-manifestation to Abraham, Moses, Joshua, and the poet-prophet Second Isaiah. Continuity and newness, covenant and promise are the unifying themes in all five lections.

Today we listen to a recital of events, a recital which took shape in the context of Israel's life of worship and which has frequently been designated a "cultic creed," one having its original setting at an ancient sanctuary, possibly Gilgal (cf. the First Lesson for the Fourth Sunday in Lent). The passage was a key one for biblical theologians of the recent past, who understood "theology as recital" and who perhaps overemphasized the idea that Deut. 26:5-11 and similar passages condense the central message of the OT into a few verses. There is a great deal of truth in that insight, but more recent scholars have rightly pointed to other strands of biblical tradition (e.g., wisdom literature) and have also warned against applying Christian terminology to such an ancient formula as this. Thus a neutral term such as *historical summary* is preferable to *cultic creed* for this firstfruits liturgical text. And although a more ancient form underlies it, it comes to us pervaded by Deuteronomic vocabulary and style.

The Deuteronomic writers are associated with the religious reforms under King Josiah in 621 B.C. One of the central features of that reformation was destruction of syncretistic places of worship in the countryside and centralization of worship at the temple in

Jerusalem. The temple is the current setting of our pericope, "the place which the Lord your God will choose, to make his name dwell there" (26:2). During the Feast of Weeks, one of three annual occasions on which the devout (or well-off?) Israelite made his pilgrimage to Jerusalem, he filled a basket with the early fruits of the harvest and took it to the temple. When a priest placed it before the altar (v. 4, but cf. v. 10b), the worshiper recited the words of vv. 5–10a.

The recital encapsules the three acts in the drama of Israel's past—the journeys of the patriarchs (v. 5), the Egyptian bondage and liberation (vv. 6–8), and the settlement in the promised land (v. 9). In response to these great events the worshiper brings his offering to the Lord. He is then enjoined to "rejoice in all the good" which God has given him.

Two details in the passage are of special note for understanding how a worshiper—one engaged in what seems to be essentially an individual cultic act of thanksgiving—was taught to interpret that trip to the temple. The plural "us" and "we" of vv. 6ff. indicate that the self-understanding of this person is rooted in the family past (cf. Deut. 6:21ff., "*we* were Pharaoh's slaves in Egypt"). And from the taproot to the past, Israel's faith leafs out in the present to include not only members of the worshiper's household but also Levites and sojourners (v. 11).

The duties and social position of the Levites fluctuated during Israel's history but at the time of Deuteronomy they were fully occupied in priestly duties and specifically forbidden to own land (cf. Deut. 18:1–8). The term *sojourners* applied to resident aliens. They did not have full civil rights in ancient Israel, but they did have protection under the law, and are classed with widows and orphans as worthy of special programs of social welfare (as in Deut. 14:28–29) and also (as here in v. 11) of a share in Israel's bounty of joy from the Lord.

Second Lesson: Rom. 10:8-13. In the midst of that great parenthesis in his Letter to the Romans where he wrestles with the question of the salvation of Israel (9—11), Paul draws again the contrast between the way of faith and the way of the law—a contrast central to his whole understanding of the gospel. The key ideas of this passage have already been expressed succinctly in 3:21–22. Here he is trying to show some of the ways in which "the law and the prophets bear witness" (3:21) to the true path to salvation. His argument rests on quotations from Deuteronomy, Isaiah, and Joel.

The first of these OT citations, Deut. 30:12–14, was introduced in 10:6. Paul reinterprets that section of the Torah as a reference to Christ. What does Scripture say? That "the word is near you, on your lips and in your heart." The structure of that verse determines Paul's rhetoric in vv. 9–10, with its seeming disjunction between what is said with the lips and believed in the heart. In fact, the terms are virtually interchangeable. The *word of faith* which Paul proclaims is *Christ*. He is ultimately the one who is near.

V. 9 links together what Barth called "the utterly unconditioned" and "the utterly strange," the lordship of Christ and the resurrection. "Jesus is Lord" was one of the earliest formulas used by the Christian community, possibly already in baptismal professions of faith. Whether or not Paul is alluding to such a confession with the lips, he was certainly acquainted with that recognized pre-Pauline formulation (cf. Phil. 2:11; 1 Cor. 12:3). To Hellenistic ears, the title *Lord (kyrios)* was a familiar one (cf. 1 Cor. 8:5–6). To Paul it emphasized his status as slave of his Lord and Master (cf. Rom. 1:1–4). The concluding verses of chaps. 5, 6, 7, and 8, as Nygren has pointed out, indicate how important a relational title Paul made it. Essential to recognition of that lordship, however, is the fact of the resurrection. Jesus is Lord because "God raised him from the dead." When a person puts heartfelt trust in that act of God, there is assurance that salvation will follow. Characteristically, Paul uses the future tense when speaking about salvation. It is not yet fully experienced.

The RSV gratuitously introduces *man* into v. 10; it is not in the text. A more accurate rendering is "For faith works in the heart to produce righteousness, confession in the mouth to produce salvation" (Barrett). It has the additional merit of retaining the Pauline idea of *faith*, which can so easily be confused with the notion of believing propositions, given the limitations of English. Again, for Paul, justification and salvation are not separable acts—one associated with lips and the other with hearts. They are two aspects of the totally reoriented life which God in Christ initiates.

At this point Paul quotes again the verse from Isa. 28:16 which he had earlier quoted (9:33). He shares a common early Christian understanding of the "stumbling block" texts to help explain Jewish rejection of the Messiah (cf. 1 Cor. 1:23; 1 Pet. 2:6–8). His point is that because of God's gift in Christ, everyone will be able to stand upright before God at the final day, and everyone is presently empowered in faith to receive the manifold gifts of God. The idea of nearness in v. 8 is the first cousin of the idea of calling upon God in v. 12. Both phrases suggest the close relationship with Christ open to the worshiper. Paul caps his demonstration that the law and the prophets bear witness to Christ with a final quotation from Joel 2:23—the same prophetic passage quoted by Peter on Pentecost (Acts 2:21). He thereby asserts, to use Barth's fine phrase, "a universalism of grace."

Gospel: Luke 4:1–13. Four matters of special interest to Luke are apparent in his distinctive treatment of the temptation story. Since the Gospels for all five Sundays in Lent are drawn from his version of the gospel, one of the aims of the exegeses will be to highlight features of Luke's own theological interpretation of the good news as that is reflected in the readings. In two cases we will be dealing with special Lucan materials: in the others there are significant differences from Matthew's use of the same material or idiosyncratic changes in Mark's. Here his interest in the role of the Holy Spirit is evident. So also is his conviction that bread is important, although not all-important. Luke attaches great symbolic significance to the city of Jerusalem, and he is acutely conscious of the importance of time. Both of these motifs emerge when one compares his treatment of the temptation with that of the other synoptics.

In 4:1 Jesus is described as "full of the Holy Spirit" when he is led *in* (not by) the Spirit for forty days in the wilderness. Luke has already mentioned the Holy Spirit in connection with John the Baptist (1:15), Mary (1:35), Elizabeth (1:41), Zechariah (1:67), and Simeon (2:26). In each case, however, the visitation of the Spirit appears to be a temporary one for a specific purpose, chiefly to inspire prophecy. Luke emphasizes Jesus' special relationship with the Holy Spirit by insisting in his baptism account that the Spirit descended "in bodily form" (3:22). Now he suggests that the indwelling Spirit continues to be with Jesus in a special way throughout his temptation experience, as well as in his subsequent ministry of proclaiming the good news (cf. 4:18).

After eating nothing for the forty days (a traditional way of saying a long time, but with a deliberate echo here of Israel's forty years in the wilderness), Jesus has three encounters with the devil. Each of the three temptations he resists is summarized by a quotation from Deuteronomy. But Luke's order differs from that of Matthew, and so does his first quotation. He shortens the phrase from Deut. 8:3b (or else Matthew expands it). In either case the emphasis here is just on the insufficiency of bread alone, not on the superiority of the word of God, as in Matthew. Whether he is using a more primitive form of Q which Matthew has elaborated, or whether he dropped half of the quotation, the result is the same. Luke shows a special concern for the physically hungry throughout his Gospel (cf., e.g., 6:21, 25), but he knows that Jesus' mission is not just to physical needs *alone*.

The second temptation according to Luke is the one in which the devil takes Jesus up and shows him the whole inhabited earth, offering him worldly power and glory. The view that the world is under the authority of the devil (6b) reflects a political pessimism common to apocalyptic thought. Jesus answers with a quotation from Deut. 6:13, pointing to the ultimate source of all authority.

Intentionally or not, Luke's order heightens the dramatic tension of the narrative, for now even the devil cites Scripture (vv. 10, 11; Ps. 91:11–12). The temptation to jump off the temple in *Jerusalem* appears to be the temptation to use his extraordinary powers to effect his mission. Luke here anticipates the decisively different way Jesus acted when he "set his face to go to Jerusalem" (9:51; cf. 9:31).

All three synoptics set the temptation story after the baptism and immediately before Jesus begins his public ministry. The Q version undoubtedly shows Christian reflection on the nature of that ministry and makes the wilderness experience a period of vocational decision. His messiahship would meet none of the popular expectations of what the Messiah could and should do. Luke puts the radical difference in italics by his distinctive ending of the narrative. The devil, he says, has "ended every temptation," but he departs from Jesus only "until an opportune time" (*kairos*, v. 13). It would seem probable that the evangelist invites us to anticipate the experience in Gethsemane. It is noteworthy, in support of that thesis, that he here omits the ministering angels of Mark 1:3 and Matt. 4:11. He alone introduces an angel to strengthen Jesus in the garden (22:43).

HOMILETICAL INTERPRETATION

There are no immediately obvious connections among the three texts assigned for this day. The First Lesson includes a recital of the mighty acts of God in ancient Israel's past life. This recital is a confession of faith that God has acted. In the Second Lesson there is also a confession that Jesus is Lord and this is so because God raised him from the dead. The Gospel is Luke's temptation story that tells of his proleptic victory over Satan.

First Lesson: Deut. 26:5-11. There is both reflection and perception in this text. It is understood by many commentators to be the liturgy for the offering of the firstfruits of the harvest at the temple in the Feast of Weeks. We may use it to reflect upon what God has done to deliver his people and to fulfill the promise made to the patriarchs of Israel to give them the land. The text rehearses the leading hand of God in the lives of the patriarchs, the saving hand of God in the Exodus, and the giving hand of God in the conquest of the land. This recital provides the context in which the worshiper offers the thanksgiving gift to the Lord for his continued provision of the fruits of the land.

Biblical faith has a deep sense of historical consciousness. The communities that produced the biblical witness were always cognizant that there was a long history of God's gracious dealings with his people. This awareness undergirded and helped them interpret their present situation under God's care. Such a historical consciousness is often absent in the contemporary American church. In many congregations there is little sense of belonging to a community with a long history behind it, and specifically a long history of God's involvement with his people.

In Lenten reflection on this text, the preacher can help the congregation rediscover the historical sense of the church whose life with God stretches for centuries. The "we" and "us" of vv. 6ff. incorporate the Israelite worshiper into the family history of Israel. By baptism the members of the church, the new Israel, are also incorporated into this same history.

The text roots the worshiper's act of dedication of the firstfruits in the recollection of God's past dealings with his people. Through thanksgiving for the whole past history of grace, the Israelite worshiper dedicated the fruits of the present harvest to God. For the church today also, the thankful recollection of God's actions through our whole history constitutes the impetus for the dedication of lives to God through loving care for our neighbors. The preacher can help the congregation perceive the dedication that is called for in the present situation of the congregation and point to some concrete instances of such dedication and thanksgiving. The shape of the life of the church is always formed by the prior activity of God.

Second Lesson: Rom. 10:8-13. If vv. 5–7 are incorporated into the reading, Paul is seen to be wrestling with the problem of whether the righteousness of humanity is based upon the works of the law or upon faith. Much in our world today seeks to build life on the basis of what we do on our own merits: the gamut runs from racial and national self-justification through financial and educational self-justification. In every case the attempt is to build lives upon shifting sands which do not withstand the onslaught of ultimate questions and problems. The preacher can help the hearers look at their own lives of self-justification in order to clear the ground for the proclamation of God's unconditional grace in Jesus Christ.

The text moves to God's act in Christ, which justifies and saves all people. The language of justification, it is true, is no longer powerful and creative for modern people. The preacher needs to search for new images which can speak with power of what God has done for his people to bring them into a loving and caring relationship with himself. The text says the "word is near you" (v. 8), which means that Christ is near to all people in the Word. His presence brings God into the lives of people, with an unconditional promise of love. This God-established relationship is faith, which enables the believer to confess the lordship of Jesus and thus to live the life of a faithful servant to the Lord.

This faith relationship is not static existence. Paul usually speaks of salvation in the future tense (see exegesis), and there is thus a dynamic quality to this new life of righteousness through faith. God has not set the relationship between himself and his people in concrete and steel. Something is yet to be. Because Jesus is risen, he continually comes in surprising ways, calling his people into new paths of obedience and truth.

Another possibility for preaching from this text is to focus on the universality of God's love, which creates a universal community of believers. There is no distinction among persons in the household of faith. God's unconditional love is poured freely upon all persons regardless of race, nationality, sex, economic status, or any worldly distinction. There is no barrier between God and humankind. He loves all alike and thus breaks down all barriers that exist among and between human beings.

A third possibility for preaching from this text is to focus on the confession that Jesus is Lord. This is the earliest confessional statement of the church and rests upon the belief that God raised Jesus from the dead and thus made him Lord (see exegesis). What does it mean for the contemporary church to confess that Jesus is Lord? How is the lordship of Jesus made manifest in the life of the world and the church today? Where is the lordship of Jesus manifested? If Jesus is Lord and the church is his servant people, then what does this mean for the life of God's people as they live in today's world?

Gospel: Luke 4:1-13. The temptation story in the Gospel according to Luke shows Jesus, confronted by the devil, wrestling with the question of his own identity and the nature of the mission given to him by God. Behind Luke's concern for the story of the temptation of Jesus as it was handed down in the tradition could lie the reality that Luke's church also was facing the same temptation in its own life. The preacher might show that even today the church faces these temptations. Who are we? How are we to do our task as God's people? The same questions constantly face the church of God in every age or situation.

The devil tests Jesus by questioning his identity. "If you are the Son of God . . ." The phrase raises the identity crisis crucially. In the Third Gospel, an account of the baptism of Jesus and a genealogy which traces Jesus' descent from God himself precede the temptation story. In both the baptism story and the genealogy it is stated clearly that Jesus is the Son of God for Luke and the church to which he writes. Then immediately in this temptation story, that identity is radically called into question. He is asked to prove who he is, as in *Jesus Christ Superstar*, when Herod wants Jesus to prove his divinity:

> Prove to me that you're divine—change my water into wine
> That's all you need do and I'll know it's all true

Prove to me that you're no fool—walk across my swimming pool
If you do that for me then I'll let you go free.

In none of the three confrontations with Satan does Jesus succumb to the temptation to validate his identity by seeking his own security or his personal power or his self-preservation.

These same temptations still face the church of Jesus Christ. There is the temptation to build security and identity in bigger buildings and self-serving programs. There is the temptation to seek personal power by letting the world and others outside the church dictate the church's task. There is the temptation to preserve itself by seeking to be on the "right" side of any issue, always the safe and and secure side. Who are you, church? Are you God's people called to love, serve, and stand with the dispossessed, the weak, the powerless, giving up your own life as God's sons and daughters for others? Or are you someone else?

The devil tempts Jesus to take the shortcut, to achieve the commissioned task by some means other than that of suffering and dying in love for all people. Jesus is tempted to feed himself on bread alone, to gain all the authority and power of earth simply by acknowledging the authority of the devil, and to make God produce the miracle of saving him when he casts himself down from the tower of the temple in Jerusalem. There is no need to perform the task given to you by God as he wants you to do it. Take the short cut and do it your own way. You can bypass the conflict and tension with the religious leaders; you can avoid the suffering and the pain of death on the cross.

The church is also faced with the temptation to take the shortcut. God's people are always tempted to bypass the way of the cross. Surely, we say, the church's mission does not have to involve witnessing to God's love and mercy. Surely there is no need to become wrapped up and involved with all of that theological jargon and gibberish. After all, the church is a nice community where people feel comfortable and make new friends and have nice experiences. Let's not disturb it with a lot of God-talk and concern for relationship with God. The church also faces the test of not being concerned about the needs of others. It is continually tempted to be concerned only about its own well-being: to seek all the pomp and power of earthly status but to deny that God is the Lord of all. The church is tempted to become the people of the gaudy and marvelous miracle, thereby proving that it has the power to do everything. The church constantly faces the temptation to bypass the cross, to become successful rather than faithful.

Jesus does not yield to the temptations of the devil. He withstands the testing in the wilderness. He wins a battle with the devil that foreshadows the ultimate victory won on the tree of the cross. The text says that the devil left him "until an opportune time." The devil reappears in Luke's Gospel in the Passion narrative when he enters into Judas to betray Jesus and thus begin the final struggle between Jesus and the devil. However, Luke also says that Jesus wins the battle not through his own strength but because the Holy Spirit filled him (v. 1). Luke also says in v. 14 that "Jesus returned in the power of the Spirit into Galilee." This bracketing of the temptation story by the references to the Spirit indicates that Jesus withstood the testing because of the ministry and power of the Spirit.

The church can withstand its own temptation to doubt it is God's people, called to be a people who suffer and die with and for others. The church is enabled to endure the temptations that come to it because Jesus has won the final victory over the devil in his death and resurrection, and because the Holy Spirit has been poured into the life of the church by God (see Acts 2). That Spirit empowers the church to be God's people, faithful to their calling.

The Second Sunday in Lent

Lutheran	Roman Catholic	Episcopal	Pres/UCC/Chr	Meth/COCU
Jer. 26:8-15	Gen. 15:5-12, 17-18	Gen. 15:1-12, 17-18	Gen. 15:5-12, 17-18	Gen. 15:1-12, 17-18
Phil. 3:17—4:1	Phil. 3:17—4:1 or 3:20—4:1	Phil. 3:17—4:1	Phil. 3:17—4:1	Phil. 3:17—4:1
Luke 13:31-35	Luke 9:28b-36	Luke 13:(22-30) 31-35	Luke 9:28-36	Luke 13:22-35

EXEGESIS

First Lesson: Gen. 15:1-12, 17-18. Promise and covenant are the great themes of this narrative. God twice takes the initiative to make himself known to Abram. He assures the patriarch that his own flesh and blood will be his heirs and that the land will be theirs.

In the symbolism of the covenant ritual, the Lord himself is the one who guarantees his promises.

Several sources are interwoven in the passage, not always smoothly. The awkwardness is apparent when you consider that it is nighttime in v. 5 and later on Abram is waiting for the sun to go down (v. 12). For our present purpose it can be divided into two sections: vv. 1–6, with major emphasis on Abram's faith, and vv. 7–12, 17–18, with major emphasis on Yahweh's faithfulness. The verses which have been omitted (13–16) are from yet another source, explaining the long delay in inheriting the land.

V. 1 begins in a manner more familiar in prophetic writings than in the Pentateuch: "the word of the Lord" comes to the patriarch in a vision, identifying himself as Abram's shield. This metaphor for Yahweh's protective activity is frequent in the Psalms, as in Ps. 59:11, for example—"O Lord, our shield." Here it underlines the fact that Abram has no need to fear this strange vision of the night.

Since Abram has no children, the promise of very great reward evokes his skepticism. The Hebrew of v. 2 is obscure, but the meaning is clarified by v. 3 and by archaeological evidence from Nuzi. It was a common legal practice in the ancient Near East for childless persons to adopt a slave to take care of them in their old age and, in turn, to become their heir. Yahweh answers Abram's skepticism with a demonstration which implies his great creative power (v. 5). He shows Abram the thousands upon thousands of stars which spangle the night sky and declares that the childless man's offspring will be as many as that uncountable host.

Because for St. Paul it was a key to understanding justification by faith and the pivot of his argument in Romans 4 and Galatians 3, the next verse (6) has played a decisive role in Christian theology. Here the response of Abram to the Lord's promise is tersely stated; he put his faith or trust in the Lord, in spite of the fact that from his human perspective the promise seemed impossible of fulfillment. That trust puts him in the right personal relationship with the Lord. Righteousness, as von Rad has shown, is not an absolute norm but a term of relationship.

A new narrative begins in v. 7, with a new self-identification on Yahweh's part. He is the one who brought Abram out from Ur of the Chaldeans (cf. 11:31). Once again Abram expresses his doubts. How can he be sure that he really will receive a new land? The covenant ceremony which follows is part of the oldest patriarchal tradition and it is full of obscurities. The closest biblical parallel is Jer. 34:19ff., but there are illuminating references in tablets found at Mari and at Hittite sites. The parties to a covenant evidently passed between the severed pieces of the animals to seal the pact, and invoked upon themselves the fate of those animals should the pact be violated. The special role of the turtledoves, pigeons, and vultures in the account is not known. Some commentators see the last ("birds of prey," v. 11) as an allusion, in this ancient tale, to an evil omen.

What follows after the preparation is pervaded by a great sense of the numinous. The "deep sleep" (v. 12) which falls on Abram is one from which he was probably awakened in awe and dread (cf. Job 4:13). It is stretching the text to translate this difficult verse as a trance (JB, Jewish Publication Society). Whatever his state of consciousness, what Abram sees are the signs of Yahweh's presence. The "smoking pot" (or portable earthenware oven) and the "flaming torch" are comparable to the pillar of cloud by day and the pillar of fire by night with which the Lord led his people in the wilderness. In this covenant ceremony, the Lord takes upon himself a unilateral obligation. No reciprocal responsibilities are here imposed on Abram.

The gift of the land is defined in the closing verses in terms of the boundaries of Solomon's empire at its greatest extent. Rather than the term "river of Egypt," suggesting the Nile, the text is properly emended to "wadi of Egypt" (v. 18) as in the JB translation. The appended list of all the names of ancient peoples known to the Israelites is probably a later addition. Their homelands were not all in the territory just described.

Second Lesson: Phil. 3:17—4:1. This lesson comes from a section of Paul's Philippian correspondence (3:2—4:3, 8) which may originally have been part of a separate letter, written on an occasion different from that of the earlier chapters. Paul is concerned to denounce specific misinterpretations of the Christian life (v. 18; cf. v. 2 and the Second Lesson for the Fifth Sunday in Lent) and to impress the readers with the need to follow his teaching and example.

He makes three contrasts in these five verses: between friends and enemies of the cross of Christ, between those who set their minds on earthly and on heavenly things, and between our present limited bodies and the body of glory which is Christ's. He ends with a characteristic "therefore," an exhortation to remain anchored in the Lord.

"The enemies of the cross of Christ" (v. 18) are almost certainly Christians who are misusing their new freedom in the gospel in a libertine, antinomian way. Eating and drinking and making merry are by implication the chief preoccupation of these people, many in number. Their manner of life is destined for nothingness. It is doubtful whether Paul would speak with such passion of those who were not already members of the Christian community.

The contrast is with the way in which Paul and his fellow workers "live" (literally "walk," v. 17). They provide a model which the Philippians should copy. The NEB in translating "brethren" as "friends" rightly brings out the comparison Paul is making here. Whereas enemies of the cross are going in the wrong direction, the people going in the right direction will be called friends of the cross. This translation further recognizes that Paul is addressing both women and men, as his appeal to Euodia and Syntyche (both of whom have worked hard with him to spread the gospel) makes explicit in the following verses (4:2–3).

Those who walk in the same direction as Paul and his co-workers have already become naturalized citizens of God's realm. The present tense in v. 20 is important: "our commonwealth *is* in heaven." This Pauline antithesis between those who are oriented toward heaven and those who are oriented toward earth is closely connected with his frequent contrast between walking according to the flesh and walking according to the Spirit (e.g., Gal. 5:16ff.). The underlying thought is not a dualism between this world and another, and emphatically not one between the body and the soul. Rather (as Bultmann so well demonstrated), Paul is talking about two alternative attitudes toward life, two opposite trajectories of the total self.

Such a reading is reinforced by Paul's final contrast in this passage (v. 21). When the Savior comes *from* heaven, he says, it will be with power to transform or refashion our present bodies and make them conformed to his own. Paul expresses a similar notion in 1 Corinthians 15, in his comparison of "animal body" and "spiritual body." We remain embodied selves at the Parousia, but with bodies of a radically different sort. We do not become resuscitated corpses.

Since Paul and the Philippian Christians are already in the Lord

(4:1), members of his body, they can eagerly anticipate his return in glory (3:20). In the interim before the Lord establishes his rule over all things, they can remain confidently grounded in the source of love. Paul ends on a note of intimacy that recalls his special affection for this the first congregation of Christians he founded in Europe. The fervent tone of 4:1 is captured in the free translation of TEV, "how dear you are to me and how I miss you! How happy you make me, and how proud I am of you!"

Gospel: Luke 13:22–35. Luke has here put together a collection of primarily Q material in such a way that he equates Jesus' teaching about acceptance or rejection of the eschatological gift of the kingdom with acceptance or rejection of Jesus as Lord. That the structure of this section is his own is indicated by the widely differing contexts in which Matthew uses the same teachings, by the appearance of his own special source material in vv. 31–33, and by the obviously editorial contribution of the rather flabby opening verse. Luke's Jesus has been en route to Jerusalem, of course, since 9:51; but the journey was not taken as the crow flies. The unitive theological theme in this pericope is essentially a call to decision.

The anonymous questioner of v. 23 asks a theoretical question. Typically, Jesus fails to answer it in the terms in which it was posed. He never seems to favor theological speculation. Rather, he begins talking about a narrow door. In Matthew the narrow opening is a gate (7:13). It is possible that Luke has changed the saying to conform to the closed door he goes on to talk about in v. 25ff. In either case, the message is clear that entry into the kingdom is not automatic. The implication is that we may be too fat to squeeze through the door.

In the following verses (25–28), Luke uses language which appears in the Matthean parable of the wise and foolish virgins (25:10–12) as well as in Matt. 22:23 and 8:11–12. The shut door theme is in curious tension with the parables of the friend at midnight in Luke 11:5–8 and of the readily opened door in Luke 12:36ff. Here, however, Luke insists that it is completely possible to confront a locked door, and that no claims to previous acquaintance with the Lord in his day as a hometown rabbi (v. 26) will unlock that door. Decisions, it appears, can be irrevocable. A quotation from Ps. 6:8 rams the point home (v. 27).

If evildoers can find themselves excluded from the messianic banquet (the first-century idiom for the Thanksgiving dinner), however, mere inherited privilege is not the basis for a guaranteed seat at the table. Luke's universalism is clear in v. 29, which is not found in the Matthean parallel. He pictures Abraham, Isaac, and Jacob around that heavenly table, along with *all the prophets*; but people from all four corners of the earth are also seated there. That imagery of a global invitation is a fitting prelude to his use of the saying about the surprising upset, the ultimate disrespect for queuing up and taking one's turn, which is expressed in v. 30, as well as in Mark 10:31 and twice in Matthew. That God does not always act in ways that we expect is firmly attested in the synoptics.

Herod the tetrarch of Galilee is then introduced in the unit from Luke's special source, which is glued on rather awkwardly with the phrase "at that very hour." We are never supposed to forget the urgency of Jesus' move toward Jerusalem, which for Luke is the center of the universe and the place toward which and from which salvation history flows. The Pharisees who bring the warning are not necessarily to be interpreted as insincerely trying to get Jesus out of their territory; they could have been honestly befriending him. The incident is used as the occasion for a saying reminiscent of Marcan predictions of the Passion (cf., e.g., Mark 8:31). It provides Luke with an opportunity for introducing Jesus' lament over Jerusalem, which Matthew more logically uses after the Palm Sunday entry into the city (Matt. 23:37–39).

Recent commentators have rightly stressed the tender, "feminine" imagery in these verses (34–35). Jesus is in no way bound by patriarchal figures of speech, by a one-sided view of himself or of his Father. He here compares himself to a mother hen wanting to embrace and protect all of her chicks. The language is close to that of Ps. 36:7, "How priceless is your love, O God! Your people take refuge under the shadow of your wings." Yet here is appended the poignant "and you would not." Luke thus reinforces the idea of human freedom and responsibility for decision which underlies this whole pericope. God in Christ invites us to enter the door, to sit at table in the kingdom, to hide under protecting wings. What is required of us at this very hour, according to the concluding verse, is responsive and glad recognition of the one "who comes in the name of the Lord."

HOMILETICAL INTERPRETATION

The three texts assigned for this day appear to have a common theme running through them. That theme is stated in a half-verse from the Gospel for the day: "How often would I have gathered your children together as a hen gathers her brood under her wings, and you would not!" (Luke 13:34b). Here is pictured the unrelenting grace of God constantly coming to humankind and the unrelenting rejection of God and opposition to his presence by those to whom he comes, particularly those persons who call themselves the people of God.

All three texts clearly proclaim the coming of God to his people in his love and grace. In the First Lesson, Yahweh comes to Abram who is childless and landless, a particularly desperate situation for an ancient nomad. The coming of God is not to destroy or terrify but rather to bind Abram to himself in love and gracious care. God comes to Abram and promises the fulfillment of his word. The word of promise is that Abram who is childless and landless will be the father of many peoples and will occupy and possess the land that God will give him. God here enters into covenant with Abram. The covenant is an unconditional agreement binding Yahweh to Abram. There is no demand or requirement placed upon Abram. God binds *himself* to the patriarch and promises to keep his word of promise. God is faithful, and his coming to his people is to fulfill his word.

In the Second Lesson, Paul writes the church at Philippi and speaks of the church's expectation of the coming of a Savior, the Lord Jesus Christ, in his eschatological glory. Paul says that God is faithful and the Lord Jesus will come in power to make his people new creatures to live in his heavenly kingdom in which they already have their citizenship.

In the Gospel, Luke continues his story, begun in 9:51, of Jesus' journey to Jerusalem. The movement to Jerusalem will end in Jesus' death on the cross, and from Jerusalem God's salvation history will flow to the whole world. In Jesus, God comes inviting his people into his kingdom to sit and eat at table with all humankind. The coming of Jesus is God's protective gathering of his people into his feast.

The preacher can use any or all of these images of God's coming to his people to stimulate the mind for contemporary experiences and images of the faithfulness of God who comes to his people to give them life and salvation. God's chief desire is to gather all people under his wings in order to provide protection, safety, and meaning for their lives. The whole biblical witness has running through it this brilliant strand of the faithful God who constantly seeks out his people to give them blessing and hope.

The reaction of humankind to God's gracious coming is so often rejection and opposition. Abram sees his situation only from his own perspective. He knows only his childlessness and that his heir is one of his slaves. His reaction to God's word to him is one of incredulity. He simply cannot believe God's word, concerning either progeny or the land. Abram asks God for proof that God will keep his word and fulfill the promise.

In the Second Lesson Paul writes of some members of the Philippian church who have experienced the coming of God into their lives but who have become enemies of the cross of Christ and have thus rejected God's presence in their lives. These enemies of the cross of Christ seem to be those who have used their Christian liberty as license, and have made their own god and denied the lordship of Jesus Christ in their lives.

In the Gospel, the long series of sayings in vv. 23–30 also portray many persons to whom God has come and who have turned away from him and his invitation to enter into his kingdom and feast with him. The rejection of God is also pictured in Herod's desire to kill Jesus. The saying about Jerusalem's killing the prophets and stoning those sent to her also paints a picture of humankind's rejection of God's gracious coming.

The task of the preacher is to illuminate the contemporary rejections of God's coming to his people. Even today, the very ones who claim to be God's people within the household of faith reject him. What are the false gods that have been created by your people? How and where do they perceive things only from their limited perspective and thus deny for themselves that God's promise can be fulfilled? Where are the contemporary invitations to God's banquet being given to the congregation, and how are they rejecting them? The task is not to scold the congregation but to help illumine for them, for the preacher's own self, the continual human rejection of God's passionate and loving coming to his people.

One should not forget that God comes to his people in and through other human beings. This mode of God's coming then allows the possibility of using human relationships to mirror and image the human opposition and rejection that is so common.

There is a third aspect in all these lessons that needs to be highlighted. This aspect is the accepting response by some of God's people to his coming into their lives. In the First Lesson, God comes and overcomes Abram's questioning skepticism by bringing Abram into relationship with himself. In the Second Lesson, the hope of Christ's coming enables God's people to live now as friends of the cross of Christ and to imitate Paul in his Christian life-style. In the Gospel, Luke faces his church with the possibility of decision in responsibility to God's gracious invitation to eat and drink at his feast, and in human freedom. In Christ's coming, God invites his people to be with him in his kingdom. The very coming of God in Christ Jesus enables the human being to respond in faithful and obedient acceptance and recognition of the one who comes in the name of the Lord.

Here is the positive side of the human response to God's desire to gather his children together under his protective wings. One of the difficulties of the present church situation is the lack of positive examples of Christian discipleship for people to imitate. Paul does not say very much about the specifics of the life-style the Philippians are to imitate in him. However, Paul does urge imitation of Abraham by his readers in other epistles as a model of faithfulness. Who are the contemporary saints of God that you can hold before your people? Who mirrors and models faithful and obedient response to the gracious invitation of the coming God for his people? Who shows us how to enter into relationship with him, to be friends of the cross of Christ, to enter the door and sit at table in the kingdom, and to be gathered under his protective wings?

The passionate seeking of God for his people and their passionate rejection and opposition is the recurring story of God's love for his people. The miracle is that God does not give up in the face of repeated rejection, but rather he comes, and keeps coming, to his people because he is the faithful one who has bound himself to his people in Jesus Christ, *and he keeps his promises*!

The Third Sunday in Lent

Lutheran	Roman Catholic	Episcopal	Pres/UCC/Chr	Meth/COCU
Exod. 3:1–8b, 10–15	Exod. 3:1–8a, 13–15	Exod. 3:1–15	Exod. 3:1–8, 13–15	Exod. 3:1–15
1 Cor. 10:1–13	1 Cor. 10:1–6, 10–12	1 Cor. 10:1–13	1 Cor. 10:1–12	1 Cor. 10:1–13
Luke 13:1–9	Luke 13:1–9	Luke 13:1–9	Luke 13:1–9	Luke 13:1–9

EXEGESIS

First Lesson: Exod. 3:1–15. In its present form, the call of Moses here presented is both the fruit of high narrative skill and "flaming with historical revelation" (Buber). Although at least J and E sources are involved, as well as the ancient oral traditions behind them, overconcern with some of the difficulties of the text can obscure the consummate artistry of the storyteller. The unit recalls the covenant with Abraham in last week's reading and adds a new thrust toward the future. It welds together corporate and personal experience. It juxtaposes the ordinary and extraordinary. In all three dimensions it is exemplary of biblical faith.

As a call narrative, the unit contains the basic elements of confrontation common to other prophetic calls such as that of Gideon in Judges 6 or of Jeremiah 1: commission, objections, reassurance, and sign. Moses encounters Yahweh at *the* holy mountain (vv. 2–6); he is told to go to Pharaoh (vv. 7–10); he protests that he is inadequate (v. 11); he is promised the Lord's companionship; he is given a sign which points both backward and forward (v. 12). There follows the revelation of the divine name in a second framework of objection and reassurance (vv. 13–15).

Brevard Childs has rightly stressed the everydayness of the opening verse. Moses is going about his daily business of finding forage for his father-in-law's flock. (The use of the name Jethro for that Midianite and of Horeb for the mountain are hallmarks of the Elohist tradition.) In the midst of that probably boring work, Moses sees "a great sight" (v. 3) and goes to look. Just such magnetic attraction is one pole of every authentic encounter with the holy, in Otto's classic analysis. The other pole—stand back, be careful, don't look too closely—is evident in 6b.

Rationalistic and psychologizing efforts to explain this event have, in the not-too-distant past, led to absurd reductionism. The burning bush was not a New England maple in full autumn glow, nor was Moses necessarily overwhelmed by the desert solitude. Similarities of sound link the thornbush (*seneh*) with the other name for the same holy mountain (*Sinai*), but it is far more important to note the other instances in which flame and fire are symbols of Yahweh's presence (cf. the Second Sunday in Lent above). The messenger in v. 2 becomes God himself in v. 4. From the midst of that extraordinary bush, God addresses Moses by his own personal name (v. 5).

This call opens what Buber called "the great duologue" which is the heart of the passage. Yahweh identifies himself in stereotyped language as the God of covenant and promise (vv. 6–8), but with a distinctive personal note in v. 6 which the NEB has emended to read "forefathers," following the Samaritan text. The MT reads "your father," meaning Moses' own parent (cf. Exod. 18:4). That reading helps bind together the individual and corporate experiences which are equally affirmed in this narrative.

God's charge to Moses evokes his first protest: Who, me (v. 11)? The promise "I will be with you" is the first half of God's response, a promise that may well give proleptic content to the cryptic v. 14. The second half is the "sign" given. Syntactical problems in v. 12b make it difficult to be sure what the "this" refers to. Childs has argued persuasively, on both traditio-historical and theological grounds, that it should be taken with a double referent. On the one hand "this" sign points back to the experience Moses has just had with the person and power of God. The flaming bush that does not burn up is itself a sign. On the other hand it points forward to the liberated community of Israel which will return to worship together upon the same holy mountain. Only the latter facet of the sign is presented in the RSV.

Moses next asks another question, probably a further stage of his evasive tactic (v. 13): Assuming that I do go, whom shall I say that I represent? The problems of translation and interpretation of the first part of God's answer to this one (v. 14) are such that the Jewish Publication Society version simply reproduces the Hebrew, *Ehyeh-Asher-Ehyeh.* Other modern translations note alternative readings to the one they have selected. The consensus underlying contemporary struggles with the text seems to be that the words do not support the idea that God is abstract being-itself, as in Aquinas's idea of the aseity of God, bolstered with this as a proof text. Rather they point to a God who is self-designated as active, one who will continue to accompany Moses and his people in the future.

In any case, that puzzling answer addressed to Moses alone in v. 14 is supplemented in v. 15 by the personal name which he is to relay to the people. Here is the divine Tetragrammaton itself, YHWH, the Lord. The reverence for the divine name which led to reticence about pronouncing it aloud is well known; but it is unfortunate that the NEB has chosen to render it with the hybrid transliteration *Jehovah.* To modern ears that antique title can easily reinforce a Marcionite separation of the God of the OT from that of the New. Use of the English *Lord* has both historic and theological basis. Who the Lord is is specified in the closing half of the verse by another reference to past and future. He is the God of the forefathers and the one who is to be remembered by the same name in all future generations.

Second Lesson: 1 Cor. 10:1-13. Although this passage is virtually a self-contained excursus in Paul's discussion of the problems facing the church at Corinth, it must be read in the light of his announced topic at 8:1, "Now, concerning food offered to idols . . ." The dangers of idolatry are a major theme of the reading, as is also clear from the verse which follows, "Therefore, my beloved, shun the worship of idols" (10:14).

Two major difficulties confront the modern reader of the passage. First, Paul presupposes greater knowledge of the OT than most listeners have today. He alludes in quick succession to various incidents surrounding the Exodus and subsequent wilderness wanderings, and each of these must be looked at closely. Secondly, he assumes that it is legitimate to read the OT typologically, an assumption not always shared by the modern exegete. Only by entering sympathetically into his procedure, however, can we hear what he is trying to say.

He begins by telling the Corinthians that he does not want them ignorant of what happened to "their" ancestors, a statement presupposing that the church is the true Israel. All of them were under God's protecting cloud (cf. Ps. 105:39); all of them were led safely through the Red Sea. All of them were given manna to eat and water to drink in the wilderness. When Paul says (v. 2) that they were baptized into Moses he has in mind the parallel of being baptized into Christ. There is no warrant in Jewish tradition for the phrase.

The spiritual food and drink of vv. 4–5 are similarly read back into the period of the wilderness wanderings from the present Christian experience of spiritual food and drink in the Lord's Supper. The incident of Moses' bringing water out of a rock is found both in Exod. 17:6 and Num. 20:11. The idea that the rock-fountain was peripatetic and followed the Israelites in their wanderings comes from rabbinic tradition. For Paul the connection between that water of life and Christ is more than metaphoric.

The reason for his urging them to remember their ancestors is razor-sharp in v. 5. "Most" of them were "overthrown in the wilderness." TEV takes liberties with the text but expresses Paul's blunt meaning graphically in the words "so their dead bodies were scattered over the desert." He is warning against any false sense of security which some Corinthians might feel just because they participate in the Christian sacraments.

Four warnings follow, all based on incidents from Exodus and Numbers. The quotation in v. 7 is from the account of Aaron's golden calf. The allusion of v. 8 is to a plague which killed not twenty-three thousand but twenty-four thousand (Num. 25:9). The "immorality" in question may well be fornication, as most commentators suggest; but in Numbers the harlotry with the Moabites is closely connected with bowing down to their gods (25:2). The force of Paul's warning is similar to that of Wisd. of Sol. 14:12, "The invention of idols is the root of immorality; they are a contrivance which has blighted human life" (NEB). Vv. 9 and 10 are injunctions against tempting the Lord and grumbling, neither of which has any self-evident relevance to the Corinthian situation. Conzelmann thinks that Paul has injected a piece of teaching which was already in this form before he wrote the epistle.

In vv. 11–13 the present application of these lessons from history is made. Paul and his contemporaries are in the last days (cf. 7:26, 29). Times may get worse. So far the Corinthians have not been called upon to face any severe testing; what they have gone through is just the ordinary human lot. But they must not allow themselves to develop an illusion that they are immune to danger, based on any sense that they are God's elite. Having delivered his warnings, Paul then ends on a note of comfort. Their true security rests in the faithfulness of God, a God who offers human beings his own presence in the time of temptation. Although that meaning of "the way of escape" is not stated directly in 10:13, it is in 1:9, where Paul first asserts that "God is faithful." He follows that assertion with the clause "by whom you were called into the fellowship of his Son, Jesus Christ." In 13:16 he continues discussion of the *koinonia* of Christ. Both the earlier and later sections of the letter give content to this thought in 10:13.

Gospel: Luke 13:1-9. Although the first half of this reading is about historical events and the second half is a parable, both parts are concerned with the opportunity of turning around and with the urgency of doing so before it is too late.

Since only Luke records the tragic incidents in vv. 1–4, we have no way of knowing the historical facts about them. During Pontius Pilate's ten-year governorship of Judea (A.D. 26–36) he offended the Jews on a number of occasions. Josephus tells of "large numbers of the Jews" who were killed in Jerusalem by Pilate's troops during a mob protest over the aqueduct he had paid for from the Jewish treasury. If the Galileans were killed while offering sacrifices, they were presumably in Jerusalem worshiping at the temple. The collapse of the tower in Siloam sounds like a construction accident. Archaeology has demonstrated that a tremendous amount of building took place in Jerusalem during the time of the Herods.

The point of mentioning the accidental deaths here, however, is to say that anyone can die at any moment. Those who were killed were not being punished because they were greater sinners than anyone else, a traditional view of suffering which Jesus roundly repudiates. They were no different from the rest of Jesus' listeners. The message is that we are living in urgent times (cf. 12:56), but that there is still time to turn around and accept God's offer of life under his reign.

The parable of the fig tree in vv. 6–9 accentuates these themes. God's gracious forbearance is indicated in the fact that the tree is given yet another chance to bear fruit. Although it is perhaps legitimate to assume that only males owned vineyards in first-century Palestine, the text just says that someone (*tis*) had a vineyard. The language is inclusive. Planting fig trees amidst the grapevines was good horticultural practice. The translation "gardener" rather than "vinedresser" (v. 7) certainly indicates that character's role more accurately.

The parable raises two intriguing exegetical questions, neither of which can be answered decisively. What, first, is the relationship between this exclusively Lucan parable and the comparable incident of Jesus cursing the fig tree repeated in Mark 11:12–14 and also in

Matt. 21:18–19, an event which Luke omits from his use of Mark? A number of commentators think that the parable which Luke found in his special sources is the original basis of that seemingly unreasonable act of Jesus in the other two synoptics. The parable suggests, that is, that the primitive Christian community was so thoroughly convinced of the unified importance of all that Jesus did and said (cf. Acts 1:1) that one could be assimilated to the other without embarrassment.

The other question concerns the amount of allegory legitimately to be read out of the parable. One should certainly avoid finding christological significance in such details as the "three years" that the owner has been looking for fruit. It is highly probable however that the parable, whatever its connection with Jesus' own words, is intended to speak of Israel's covenant relationship with the Lord. The ancient and pervasive scriptural metaphors of Israel as the Lord's vineyard (Isa. 5, e.g.) and the need for trees to bear fruit (cf. Luke 3:9) are inevitably awakened by such a story. God's people cannot finally escape his judgment. Nevertheless, the parable tells us, he is willing, as so many times in the past, to offer them yet another chance to respond to the loving care lavished upon them.

HOMILETICAL INTERPRETATION

Two themes emerge from a careful reading of the assigned texts for today. Both themes pose constant pastoral issues for the church, and both are intimately a part of the Lenten journey to the cross. The two themes that emerge are the mystery of suffering and the mystery of holiness. Either theme could be developed homiletically, starting with one of the assigned texts and then using the other two to illuminate and sharpen the message.

The mystery of suffering is raised in the Gospel by Jesus, who denies that each individual's suffering is the result of that person's own sin. However, in the Second Lesson Paul says that some human suffering is the result of human sin and the resulting judgment of God. The First Lesson is not concerned with the cause of suffering, but rather proclaims that God is the one who sees the suffering of his people and acts to deliver them from it. The movement toward the cross continues. In Jesus' death God has acted to take upon himself the totality of human suffering in order to deliver humankind from the burden.

The mystery of holiness is set forth in the Second Lesson by Paul. He says that the Corinthians have presumed upon God's mercy by assuming they are privileged because they have been baptized and have the sacrament of the altar. They now suppose they may live as they please. Paul says this is not so. If you play games with the Holy, you will get burned. And that is also the word of the parable in the Gospel. The loving God has given his people life, and he expects them to produce the fruits expected by him. If the fruit is not produced, then judgment will come. Yet the parable also says that God is forbearing and will yet give time for the fruit to be produced. In the First Lesson the Holy One expects distance between himself and human beings, but in his holiness he does seek to deliver his people from injustice and oppression.

First Lesson: Exod. 3:1-15. A chief temptation in this lesson is to make Moses the hero or chief actor in the story and sermon. To focus upon the call of Moses and his recurring objections to God's mission can be exciting and interesting, particularly as they are translated into contemporary experiences. However, to focus on Moses is to miss the intent of the text, which is to proclaim the action of God.

The story proclaims God's involvement and concern in the life of his people. God's concern is for justice and the breaking of oppression. This is indicated by God's saying, "I have seen the affliction of my people who are in Egypt . . . and I know their sufferings . . ." This is the essence of the biblical witness concerning God's love and care for his people. God is not a God far off but is the one who sees, hears, knows the stuff of human bondage and who comes to his people in their bondage to deliver them.

The task of the preacher is to discover and highlight the contemporary oppressions and sufferings of God's people. What are the bondages that bind people today? What are the social, public afflictions, as well as the personal, private ones, that gnaw away and dehumanize people in your community? These are the sufferings that God sees and hears and comes to heal.

God's coming to be with his people is always done in a surprising manner. Here he calls the weak Moses to be his mouthpiece, his instrument of deliverance. In Moses, God is present to help his people and to set them free from their bondage. For the New Testament witness, God becomes fully human in Jesus to suffer with and for his people in order to set them free from bondage to sin, suffering, and death. God is the one who suffers with his people and in whose suffering and weakness is the power to heal and deliver.

In what ways and through what means does God come to his people today? Where are the people and institutions today that God uses to alleviate the suffering of his people? What are your personal experiences of God's coming to you in your own suffering to help and deliver? Can these experiences give you some clues about where and how God is present in the lives and world of your people today?

The text also looks beyond the Egyptian bondage to the time of freedom. When God, through Moses, delivers his people from Pharaoh's brickyard, then they are to worship God upon the mountain. God is a dynamic God who never is static but always on the move. He is the one who came to the fathers and who comes now and continues to come. His people are also a dynamic people. When God has healed his people, then they are to worship him. In our day too, worshiping God involves us in becoming his instruments of healing and freedom for other persons in their affliction and bondage. We are called to be the means of God's healing and freeing presence in the life of our world and our neighbors. And yet we are not alone. The One who has seen our own affliction and come to heal is the One who promises that he is with us as we now take upon ourselves the suffering of others in order that they may be healed and freed.

Second Lesson: 1 Cor. 10:1-13. The exegesis notes the difficulty we may have with the way Paul uses the OT in this passage. We may not be able to read the OT christologically as Paul does, but his intention is clear. Paul recalls the history of the old Israel to illuminate the present situation of the new Israel. His is a word of warning that Christians are not to presume upon the grace of God and suppose that because they have been forgiven they can live as they please.

The concrete situation being addressed is that of a false sacramentalism in Corinth. Often such a conception is present in many of our congregations. God's forgiving grace has been poured into our lives in baptism and the Lord's Supper. By the waters of our baptism, we have been united with Christ in his death and resurrection. God's loving power has made us his own people. This does not mean that we have now become our own masters. The danger is that we shall become overconfident through a false sense of security and live as though nothing at all has been changed in our life, as though in accepting God as Lord we had not acquired new moral imperatives. The danger is that our people—and we—can begin to believe that because God loved us we are now automatically in the kingdom and cannot be separated from God.

There is, however, a real danger in this text for the preacher. The danger is that we shall put conditions upon the unconditional grace of God that Paul so clearly proclaims in his epistles. The preacher needs to be aware of the danger. Yet the reality is that the call of the gospel is that we should become what God has already made us—God's people. And in Paul's view that was not happening in Corinth. Oftentimes it does not happen in our own congregations.

Drawing upon OT stories, Paul focuses attention upon the actions of the Corinthian Christians that evidenced their failure to become what God had made them to be: idolatry, immorality, testing God, and grumbling. What are the concrete actions of your people that would indicate their presumption upon God's gracious love for them? What are the situations in your congregations that manifest a failure of your people to live out the baptismal gift of God of new life with him?

The preacher also needs to note that this text does not beat the Corinthians black and blue with the hammer of the law. Paul is very much aware that God is merciful and faithful. The promise in the text is that God will be with his people to struggle with them against every force and every power that tempts them to loosen their discipleship. God's promise to be with his people in the midst of their struggle to become what he has already made them is the essence of the gospel. We have already heard this same promise in today's First Lesson.

Gospel: Luke 13:1-9. The mystery of divine judgment meets us in this text. In vv. 1–5 Luke has Jesus reject a direct causal link between an individual's sin and his or her own suffering. The people killed by Pilate and by the fall of the tower of Siloam were not such great sinners that they were somehow being punished by death. Jesus' rejection of the causal link between sin and punishment is in close relationship to the Book of Job, which argues that specific sins are not met with specific punishments. The view that specific sins bring direct, specific judgment is alive and well in our day. Every pastor has been asked, "What did I do to deserve this?" Such a conception of sin and punishment perceives God to be a vindictive and angry deity lurking in the shadows ready to pounce upon sinful people. This view of divine judgment does not yet perceive the reality of the divine mercy rooted in the cross, which proclaims God's loving involvement in the midst of human suffering.

Yet Luke's Jesus does imply some kind of relationship between sin and judgment when he issues a call for his hearers to repent (vv. 3 and 5). Collective sin in societies and groups which organize themselves upon a foundation of violence and oppression must expect tragic consequences to follow. The parable of the fig tree clearly states that judgment will come upon those who do not produce the expected fruits, even upon the people of God. The command of the vineyard owner to cut down the fruitless tree is a word of impending judgment.

What are the injustices and oppressions that operate in your community and world that can and do lead to tragic consequences? What are the specific and clear fruits that are lacking in your people's lives and in your own life that the gospel word seems to expect from us who are baptized into the death and resurrection of Jesus? The parable does not tell us the nature of the fruits expected from the vineyard. The concrete spelling out of the fruits that are lacking can become the basis for a call to repentance to your hearers.

Still, however, the mystery of divine judgment meets us in the parable. God is pictured here not as the vindictive, angry One who wants to pounce upon us; rather he is portrayed as the One who mercifully delays the ax of judgment. God is pictured as the patient husbandman who lovingly works against everything that produces fruitlessness in the life of his people. His patience is overwhelming and he constantly offers to those upon whom he has poured his love the opportunity to repent and thus to bear the expected fruit.

The Fourth Sunday in Lent

Lutheran	Roman Catholic	Episcopal	Pres/UCC/Chr	Meth/COCU
Isa. 12:1-6	Josh. 5:9, 10-12	Josh. (4:19-24) 5:9-12	Josh. 5:9-12	Josh. 5:9-12
1 Cor. 1:18-31 or 1 Cor. 1:18, 22-25	2 Cor. 5:17-21	2 Cor. 5:17-21	2 Cor. 5:16-21	2 Cor. 5:16-21
Luke 15:1-3, 11-32	Luke 15:1-3, 11-32	Luke 15:11-32	Luke 15:11-32	Luke 15:1-3, 11-32

EXEGESIS

First Lesson: Josh. 5:9-12. God's faithfulness to his covenant promises and his providential care for his people Israel continue to be the main theme of the OT lessons for this season. By starting this reading at v. 9, the compilers of the lectionary have also stressed the fact of the divine initiative already evident in the accounts of the theophanies to Abraham and Moses. Now the Lord speaks to Joshua, the successor of Moses.

Chaps. 2—9 of the Book of Joshua contain ancient traditions associated with the sacred sanctuary of Gilgal, traditions which have subsequently been edited by a Deuteronomic writer with a distinctive outlook on his people's history. Chap. 5 immediately follows accounts of the crossing of the Jordan, described in different ways in chaps. 3 and 4. It includes three incidents which are Israel's preparation for a holy war of conquest, as Israel later interpreted it. All three bear marks of liturgical practices. In the first (vv. 2–9), the invaders are circumcised in their camp at Gilgal, near Jericho. In the second (vv. 10–12), our primary pericope, they celebrate the Passover, for which the circumcisions have now qualified them. In the third (vv. 13–15), Joshua encounters one of the Lord's ambassadors in a scene deliberately recalling Moses' encounter with the Lord in the burning bush. For the Deuteronomic editor, Joshua *is* a second Moses, and all three incidents in this chapter are firmly tied to the Exodus events.

What the Lord means by his words to Joshua in v. 9, "I have rolled away the reproach of Egypt," is not at all clear. In context it appears to be his seal of approval on their newly circumcised condition; but since the original male refugees from Egypt are all explicitly said to have been duly circumcised (5:5) before they left, there seems little reason for blaming the stigma of uncircumcision on the Egyptians. Nevertheless it is certain that this phrasing, "rolled away," provides a chance to explain how Gilgal got its name. We are given an etiological explanation, based on strained etymology. We are being told that the name Gilgal comes from the Hebrew verb *galal*, "to roll," which sounds vaguely similar.

Whether or not Gilgal was ever the single central sanctuary of Israel during the period of the tribal confederacy is debated. Along with Shechem, Shiloh, and Bethel, however, it was certainly a very ancient place of worship in Israel and perhaps earlier. It was a holy place, according to one tradition, marked by twelve prominent stones. According to 1 Sam. 11:14–15, it is the place where Samuel anointed Saul to be the first king over all Israel. Probably at one time the ark was kept there.

In this narrative (vv. 10–12) Gilgal is the place where the Passover was first celebrated in Canaan. This ritual event thus formally closes the forty years of wandering in the wilderness as they had begun—with thanksgiving for Yahweh's deliverance of his people from bondage. Although the date here is probably a later addition to older material, "the fourteenth day of the month" (v. 10) is precisely the date set in the account of the first Passover in Exod. 12:6.

The account before us appears to reflect a very ancient tradition coming from a time before the Feast of Unleavened Bread was assimilated to the Passover celebration. Joshua's troops eat unleavened cakes "on the day after the Passover" (v. 11). Tradition historians think that this points to a time when a festival of bedouin origin (featuring roast lamb) was distinct from a festival of agricultural people celebrating the spring harvest. It is noteworthy that the manna, the miraculous food with which Yahweh sustained them throughout the wilderness experience, stops coming on that latter day (v. 12). The people of Israel are on the way to becoming settled in the land. Henceforth they shall eat not bread dropped daily from heaven but the Lord's grain in its time and his wine in its season (cf. Hos. 2:9).

Second Lesson: 2 Cor. 5:16-21. This lesson overlaps the Second Lesson for Ash Wednesday, and the exegetical comments on vv. 20–21 made there will not be repeated here. Even as the "so" which introduced that reading demanded a look at the larger context, so does the opening "From now on, therefore" of this lection. Over and over again in his correspondence with the church at Corinth Paul insists that the cross is the pivot of history. He has just said it once again in the words "him who for their sake died and was raised" (v. 15).

Paul asserts two consequences which follow from this death-resurrection event. First, it changes one's standards for thinking about every human being (v. 16). In the light of Good Friday and Easter, the merely human, this-worldly point of view is an inadequate one for judging any person. Paul is insisting that his whole outlook has changed. He admits that he once regarded Christ simply in that way—literally, knew Christ according to the flesh. Commentators have puzzled over when that was, and some have even suggested that he is claiming to have met the earthly Jesus. The weight of probability, however, lies with the interpretation implicit in the RSV translation. Before his conversion, Paul thought of Jesus in purely human terms. Now he looks at Christ and therefore everyone else from an angle changed by 180 degrees.

Second, the cross changes the very being of anyone who is personally related to the one who died and was raised (v. 17). The fact that anyone who is in Christ is a new creation is closely related to Paul's idea of the Second Adam, spelled out in Romans 5. The idea of the Creator's taking new initiative to rehabilitate the cosmos has already been made explicit in this letter at 4:6. Here Paul claims with a note of triumph that the new age has started. And here, as in Rom. 8:18ff., he links the idea of a total renewal of the universe to the action of God on behalf of human beings.

In the next two verses there is some confusion about the pronoun "us." Paul often switches the referent of his pronouns without warning. In 18a and 19a he is unquestionably talking about the activity of God for the sake of all humanity. (Not just for the elect, as older commentators argued.) The ideas he most wants to make sure that his readers understand are that God is the one who effected a new relationship with his creation ("all of this is from God") and that this new relationship was accomplished "through Christ." Modern translations note the difficulty of deciding where the "in Christ" of v. 19 should come. The probability is that Paul is not making a christological statement about the person of Christ, but rather an instrumental statement about the agency God used and uses to reconcile all of us to himself.

In 18b and 19b, however, the "us" taken in context appears to refer to Paul and his co-workers rather than to all Christians. This reading is strengthened by the appeal he makes, as an ambassador of Christ, to the Corinthians themselves in v. 20. Taken together, the second half of both verses closely links the "ministry" of reconciliation (service, *diakonia*) and the message (word, *logos*). For Paul, as for John, doing the truth and proclaiming the truth are two sides of the same coin. Or, in the language of reconciliation which he is here using, serving to restore relationships and announcing that they have been restored through Christ are part and parcel of the work of Christian ministry. It is as if Paul knew, before the phrase was invented, that the medium is the message.

Gospel: Luke 15:1-3, 11-32. By introducing the parable of the prodigal son with vv. 1–3, the lectionary points to the relationship between Jesus' own historical situation and that of the characters in the story. All three of the parables of chap. 15 concerning the lost (sheep, coin, son) are put together in a literary unit intended to throw light on Jesus' close association with social outcasts, and on the grumbling Pharisees who are shocked by his having table fellowship with them (vv. 1–2). Nevertheless most contemporary scholars stress the parable's own aesthetic coherence. Its meaning is to be found primarily within its own plot, not imposed on it from the setting in which Luke has placed it.

Similarly, current stress on the structure and movement of the whole story qualifies the older view that the father is the central character and indeed that the parable has been misnamed all these years—that it should have been called The Loving Father. There is, of course, an intended analogy between the behavior of the human father and the way God acts. Yet the human relationships among all three characters in the story are what give it the power it has had to change lives. Clearly we are better able to identify existentially with one of the sons.

The opening words, "a man had two sons" (v. 11), make it highly unlikely that the episode about the older brother (vv. 25–32) was tacked on later, as some have claimed. The father's response to the younger son's request for his inheritance is to divide his property between "both" of them (v. 12). Some debate persists as to the precise laws of inheritance in Jesus' day, but there is general agreement that disposal of the estate was sometimes done in this way—much as a person today might give away money before death to protect his heirs from taxes. Thus it is unfair to the story to indict the younger son, as some commentators have done, for treating his father as if he were already dead.

The story moves swiftly from home to "a far country" (v. 13), from comfort to misery. Feeding pigs would seem the most ignominious of jobs to a Jew. The young man is soon hungry enough to eat the "pods" (v. 16) of carob trees—not thought fit for human consumption. But then he comes to self-knowledge, recognizes what a fool he has been, and starts home again (vv. 17–20). To use Crossan's apt phrase, this is a parable of reversal.

The father's completely gracious behavior almost needs no further comment. He "runs" to meet the prodigal when he is "still at a distance" (v. 20). Whereas the son had hoped at best to come home as a servant, the father calls for the servants "quickly" to lavish gifts on "this my son." Whereas shortly ago the son would have been glad to eat pig food, the father provides the fatted calf. The reversal is so complete that it can only be called a change from death to life (v. 24).

Four of the details in the final episode merit attention. With superb artistry the story pictures the elder brother sulking outside and the father coming "out" to him, just as he had to the younger (v. 28). It intensifies the elder brother's self-alienation, his refusal of relationship, by the contrast between the words "this son of yours" (v. 30) and "this your brother" (v. 32). It subtly introduces the idea that the elder son's judgmental attitude goes beyond the facts of the case, by specifying "living with harlots" (v. 30) and thus embroidering the unspecific self-indulgence of v. 13. And it fills the air with music and dancing (v. 25), the proper outward and audible signs of a return from death to life.

Like all great works of art, this parable is bottomless. Commentators who find in it the whole of the Christian gospel may be stretching the literal facts but not the theological richness of the tale. Yet the dominant notes are surely those of the father's surprising invitation to both sons to come and be glad, and the freedom each has to accept or reject the invitation. Appropriately we are not told what the elder son decided.

HOMILETICAL INTERPRETATION

The mood of the assigned texts for this day is decidedly

different from that in many of our previous lessons. There is a break in our journey to the cross. Our march has been accompanied by the somber beat of the drums of judgment and repentance. Today, however, there is a note of joy and newness that accompanies our Lenten path. Each lesson speaks of an action of God that meets the needs of his people in the midst of their changed and different circumstances. The word here is promise that God will continue to be present with his people in the midst of change, to sustain and love them. The one who has shown himself to be faithful in the past is still the one who continues to manifest himself in loving, surprising ways to his people.

In the First Lesson, ancient Israel is at Gilgal. God has brought them into the land of Canaan and thus kept his promise to the fathers. Here Israel celebrates the Passover and recalls the loving action of God to free the people from Egypt's bondage. However, the situation is now radically changed. No longer are they a nomadic people on the move in the desert. Now they begin the process of settling into the land. Miraculously the manna sent from God to sustain Israel in the wilderness ceases. Now God will feed his people from "the fruit of the land of Canaan." God is ever active in new ways to meet the needs of his people.

In the Second Lesson, Paul heightens the note of God's new activity to sustain his people. The cross of Jesus produces a wholly different situation for people who have been buried with Christ and raised to new life with him in their baptism. They are "new creations." They are enabled to perceive people differently. They are enabled to carry out the new tasks given to them by God in their new situation. God makes them new and acts anew to sustain and enable his people to live creatively in their new circumstances.

The parable of the prodigal son also proclaims that God acts in very surprising ways to produce new possibilities and new relationships in the changing circumstances of our human life. The younger son returns home expecting to determine *his* own status within the family. The older son seeks to determine *his* position within the household. To our great surprise, the father in his creative love cuts through both their attempts to determine relationships. He creates a wholly new situation. The feasting of the party is God's gift that produces new situations for his people, in spite of our own attempts to become the determiners of our own existence in our Father's house.

The theme of God's ever-new actions to care for his people can be based on any one of the three lessons, and the other two used to help illuminate and sharpen the message. However, as Paul so eloquently states in the Second Lesson, it is the cross of Christ that demonstrates God's faithfulness and also his ever-new actions to meet his people in their changed circumstances. We are still on our journey to Calvary.

First Lesson: Josh. 5:9-12. Change appears to be the one constant in our life. All of us face constant changes, from new homes to new neighbors to new jobs to new situations at work or at school. Rapid change is *the* experience of our time. Even the church is not immune to it. New liturgies, new hymns, new programs, and new ways of doing things seem to put congregations oftentimes into a spin. There is something in our human condition that makes it difficult to handle change, to adapt, to be resilient. Every pastor knows this human concern and can make it vivid for the people.

Ancient Israel also experienced radical changes in its life. The story of Israel at Gilgal pictures a very radical change in life-style. They have ended their wilderness wanderings and crossed the Jordan into the land of promise. No longer are they to be homeless nomads constantly on the move. Now they begin the conquest of Canaan and will settle into this land and become farmers and village dwellers. The narrative recounts the celebration of the Passover that reminds them of God's saving love for them in the past. He delivered them from Egyptian bondage. He is faithful because he has brought them into the land. However, he will continue to be present to sustain his people in their new situation. The manna that sustained Israel in the wilderness ceases. Henceforth God will feed his people through "the fruit of the land of Canaan."

God's faithfulness and God's promise to continue to care for his people, whatever their situation, are words that people amid changing circumstances need desperately to hear. Some congregations that once were large and magnificent are now shrinking and seemingly powerless. Other congregations are faced with changing neighborhoods and different ethnic patterns emerging, and they are uncertain what they are to do. People can be helped to hear of the faithfulness of God to them in their past life. God's faithfulness then becomes the basis for a new word of God, that he has not deserted his people in their changed situation. God promises that he will continue to strengthen and sustain his people in their new "land." The preacher will want to make concrete and fleshly the activity of God to sustain his people in their present context. The preacher will also want to remind the hearers of the risen Lord's promise to be in the midst of his people, especially as they struggle with their mission to be God's servant people amidst the changing scenes of life.

Second Lesson: 2 Cor. 5:16-21. One of the amazing and consternating realities of God's dealing with his people is his constant habit of breaking into our lives and overturning our presuppositions. It seems as though we somehow manage to make our life or our perceptions safe and secure, and suddenly God appears and radically upsets and reorders things for us. Flannery O'Connor in her short story "A Good Man Is Hard To Find" states it well. Her character, Misfit, says, "Jesus is the only One that ever raised the dead . . . and He shouldn't have done it. He thrown everything off balance. If He did what He said, then it's nothing for you to do but throw away everything and follow Him, and if He didn't, then it's nothing for you to do but enjoy the few minutes you got left the best way you can—by killing somebody or burning down his house or doing some other meanness to him" (*A Good Man Is Hard to Find and Other Stories* [New York: Harcourt Brace Jovanovich, 1955]).

Paul states the same reality in this text. No longer is he able to regard anyone from a human point of view, because God has come into his life and the love of Christ controls him. (See the exegesis and 2 Cor. 5:14.) The standards for the way we regard human beings have been radically changed by the cross of Christ. The way a human being is valued and esteemed has been turned upside down because in Christ all persons are new creations. Our regard of people who are different than we—the poor or the rich, the intellectuals or the dullards, the native American or the naturalized American, the powerful or the weak (and the list could continue)—has been radically changed. That change is a consequence of the new age that has dawned in Christ's cross. The new age has changed our very being, because we have been baptized and incorporated into the death and resurrection of Jesus. The preacher's task is to make concrete and real for the hearers the reality of this new situation in the congregation being addressed. Where are the new creations in your congregation? What is your own experience of having been made a new creation and living in the new age? Can you draw upon your own changed perceptions to help your people see this activity of God?

This new perception of our situation in God's new age has implications for the ministry of the people of God. There is now no bifurcation possible between the ministry of reconciliation and the message of that action. Doing and speaking are to be congruent. We are to put our money where our mouth is. The task of God's servant people is to be agents of the restoration of relationships that have been broken, both personal and societal. The servants of reconciliation are also to announce that God has restored all broken relationships through Christ (see the exegesis). Your hearers need to be helped to see this ministry of reconciliation in its local and concrete realities. Where and how can your people incarnate the healing of broken relationships and proclaim that divine activity? It can be done, because God has made us into new creations through Christ, who reconciled us unto himself. It can be done because God is making his appeal to the world through us (see v. 20).

Gospel: Luke 15:1-3, 11-32. The parable of the prodigal son is a narrative that draws a word picture of God's gracious love for us in making us whole, in bringing us into relationship with himself, with each other, and with ourselves. The chief actor in the story is the father. Yet, as the exegesis says, existentially we can identify more closely with the two sons. The world in which we live is quite productive of prodigal situations.

The younger son's experience in the far country is the experience of many people today: the anxiety, fear, and loneliness of trying to cope inside a system that seems only to take and take and crush people into things; the emptiness and dread that gnaw at the center of our beings; and attempts to dull the pain through drugs or alcohol or sex. We are driven to be disconnected from ourselves. We become emotionally sick, or else we simply assume that life is hell and that is the way it ought to be. The preacher can aptly describe the prodigals of the congregation's experience.

The elder brother also dwells in many people today, especially people who claim to belong to the church. There are many people in our world who know where they stand and who are in touch with themselves. They are upstanding, productive members of church and society. They are able to meet the requirements of family, job, and church. But many of these persons, just like the elder brother, get very angry when the game of life is not always played according to the rules which they themselves have obeyed to secure their existence. The preacher can clearly bring the elder brothers in the lives of the hearers into flesh-and-blood reality.

What the two brothers have in common is the way they both want to control their situation, their standing within the loving circle of their father's house. The younger son wants to establish his own conditions for his return home. He will become a servant in his father's house. The elder brother seeks to maintain the properly distant, properly rigid ordering of life that he has lived in for lo these many years. The elder brother is not at all interested in getting personally involved with his father or with his brother. He seeks only to maintain the control of the relationships on his own terms.

The centrality of the father's action in the story is crucial. Notice that like a surgeon cutting out a malignant tumor he deftly cuts through the attempt of both his sons to maintain and control the relationships within his house. He does not accept the younger son's conditions of return but runs out to meet him and restores him into the full circle of sonship without conditions. He gives him the marks of sonship and throws a party for him. The father simply will not let the younger son call the shots. Likewise, the father goes out to the elder son and takes the play away from him by reminding him that the father's love and care have always been his as long as he has lived in his father's house.

The parable proclaims that God cuts through all of our attempts to regulate on our terms his personal involvement, his great love for us. The accepting, forgiving, life-restoring love of God which touches our lives and invites us into relationship with himself, with each other, and with our own selves is the party to which we are invited. God prepares this joyous feast for all people through the prodigality of spending his own Son's life for the world.

The Fifth Sunday in Lent

Lutheran	Roman Catholic	Episcopal	Pres/UCC/Chr	Meth/COCU
Isa. 43:16-21	Isa. 43:16-21	Isa. 43:16-21	Isa. 43:16-21	Isa. 43:16-21
Phil. 3:8-14	Phil. 3:8-14	Phil. 3:8-14	Phil. 3:8-14	Phil. 3:8-14
Luke 20:9-19	John 8:1-11	Luke 20:9-19	Luke 22:14-30	John 8:1-11

EXEGESIS

First Lesson: Isa. 43:16-21. This prophetic oracle is part of a longer poem in which Second Isaiah describes the impending downfall of Babylon at the hands of the conquering Persians under Cyrus the Great. He pictures in incomparable imagery the return of the Israelite exiles to their homeland, in a new exodus which makes the old one from Egypt seem pale. He asserts Yahweh's sovereignty over history and nature with dramatic force. Yahweh is once again about to liberate his people.

The first strophe opens with the traditional words, "Thus says the Lord," as in 43:14 and 44:6; but the actual words which the Lord speaks through the prophet are postponed until v. 18. First the poet identifies the One he has already called Redeemer (v. 14) with a vivid reminder of his power over the Red Sea and over the Egyptian armies. He made "a path in the mighty waters" for Israel, and he also led out the Egyptian horses and chariots. Yahweh is in control of events even when human beings are unaware of his existence (cf. 45:1, 4). Because of his activity the army was "snuffed out like a wick" (NEB).

Having just asked Israel to remember "the former things," the poet now tells them to forget them. They should not dwell upon the past, because the Lord is about to do "a new thing" (v. 19). Second Isaiah's theology of history accentuates the fact of newness. History does not repeat itself. "Behold, the former things have come to pass, and new things I now declare" (42:9). "From this time forth I make you hear new things" (48:6). The new event which is about to spring forth is so clear to the prophet's eye that he asks whether his hearers cannot already see it too.

Most modern translations of the last part of v. 19 have emended the text to conform to the reading of the DS Scroll of Isaiah, which reads *paths* rather than *rivers* "in the desert." Thus the poetic line says the same thing twice: the Lord is about to make a highway across the more than six hundred miles of desert between Babylon and Jerusalem (cf. 40:3ff.). That poetic image carries with it an implicit contrast with the wandering in the wilderness which followed the first exodus. This time, as it were, they can go straight home.

The concluding strophe (vv. 20–21) adds more detail to the prophet's vision of a transformed nature and reiterates his conviction of Yahweh's irrevocable concern for his chosen people, whom he has borne since their birth (cf. 46:3). He will create rivers in the desert so that his people can have drink. The metaphors of thirst and water in Second Isaiah are many-leveled and certainly suggest that the Lord meets both physical and spiritual needs (cf., e.g., 41:17–18). The wild beasts, specifically the jackals and ostriches which are native to the steppe, will therefore give him glory. Anyone who has seen these unattractive creatures in a zoo or who remembers the description of the ostrich in Job 39:13ff. will marvel anew at the power of this poet. *All* of creation gives glory to the Creator who calls each star by name (40:26).

Finally, the passage ends with a definition of Israel's vocation (v. 21b). The line deserves comparison with Deut. 7:7 and 9:4, with their respective answers to the question of why God so oddly chose the Jews. Second Isaiah's answer is unequivocal. He *formed* Israel for himself in order that they might sing his praise. The whole hymnic passage thus amounts to an exposition of the earlier injunction, "Sing to the Lord a new song, his praise from the end of the earth!" (42:10).

Second Lesson: Phil. 3:8–14. Once again, as on the Second Sunday in Lent, the epistle is taken from that section of Paul's letter to the Philippians which many scholars believe to be a fragment of a separate letter. Paul's mood contrasts sharply with the warmly affectionate tone which pervades the letter as a whole. This passage comes in the midst of harsh denunciation of the "dogs" who want the Philippians to mutilate their flesh. It follows immediately on an autobiographical section reminiscent of Galatians 2 and 2 Corinthians 11, where Paul boasts of his former achievements as a Jew. In this context, the loss of the things which he now counts as "garbage" (v. 8, NEB, TEV) refers to his former prestige and accomplishments in the old religious establishment. His present status is one of "surpassing worth" because it is one in which he knows Christ.

Three major themes of Pauline theology are compressed in these two paragraphs: the distinction between two types of righteousness (v. 9), the centrality of the death-resurrection event (v. 10), and the tension between present and future (vv. 12–14). Each is introduced, however, as a facet of his own personal experience with the one whom he calls "my" Lord.

Those who are "in Christ" (cf. 1:21; 2:1), Paul says, are participants through faith in the righteousness of God. They no longer need claim any righteousness of their own, based on obedience to the law. He works out the reasoning behind this contrast at greater length in Romans and Galatians. Here, almost in passing, the former Pharisee emphasizes the fact that his new freedom from the law depends on his relationship to Christ. The relational character of the righteousness he is talking about is underlined by the NEB free translation, "finding myself incorporate in him."

Paul goes on to specify more clearly that to know Christ (v. 10) involves knowing both the "power" of his resurrection and the "fellowship" of his suffering. The RSV translation obscures the fact that the clause contains two parallel nouns, *dynamis* and *koinōnia*. Because he knows the power of Christ's resurrection in his own life now, Paul knows that he may also be a partner in the self-giving love which led to the cross. The thought is very close to that which introduces the hymn of chap. 2: "Have this mind among yourselves which you have in Christ Jesus . . ."

The next three verses express the already/not yet reality of the Christian life as Paul knows it. Christ has made him his own (v. 12). That is an accomplished action. It remains for Paul fully to grow up into the new life in Christ. The double repetition of "press on" in vv. 12 and 14 and the "straining forward" of v. 13 are metaphors of the footrace. Paul thinks of himself, as it were, as coming down the homestretch. He knows that God calls to him from ahead, from the finish line. The prize, here as throughout the letter, is one of a living relationship with God in Christ (cf. 1:21–23). Although the word is not used in the text, this whole section is a strong statement of the Pauline idea of Christian hope which energizes believers.

Gospel: Luke 20:9–19. Luke is here following his Marcan source (12:1–12) closely. Yet he makes a number of changes—most of which appear to be the result of his sensitive ear as a superb storyteller, but at least one of which has theological import. First he drops the details of the hedge around the vineyard, the wine press, and the tower which Mark's version includes under the direct influence of Isaiah 5. This gets the story off to a brisk start; it may also distance it from the old Israel. Second he specifies that the absentee landowner went away for "a long while," a nice detail which heightens the subsequent drama. Third he pares down the cast of characters, eliminating the "and so with many others" of Mark 12:5. We are left with just the threesome of emissaries appropriate to good folkloric style. No one of them is killed, although each is treated more severely than his predecessor.

Thus the Lucan version is less blatantly allegorical than either Mark's or Matthew's, which appear to introduce the prophets in general and perhaps John the Baptist in particular into the story. Nevertheless, Luke along with Matthew changes the wording of Mark 12:8 to make it certain that even the dullest reader understands that the son in question is Jesus, who was killed outside of Jerusalem, outside of the vineyard which is Israel.

The decisive theological change which Luke makes in his Marcan source occurs in the quotation from Scripture which announces the triumphant vindication of the son who was killed. Both Mark and Matthew continue the quotation from Psalm 118 through v. 23, "This was the Lord's doing, and it is marvelous in our eyes." Luke, in contrast, rounds off the direct scriptural quotation with an enigmatic combination of words from Isa. 8:15 and Dan. 2:34: "If you stumble over the new cornerstone, you will be broken to pieces; if it falls on you, you will be crushed" (v. 18). The two verses may already have been conjoined in primitive *testimonia*, the fruits of early Christian searching of Scripture to interpret the Christ, but used here they turn the jubilation of Mark 12:11 into threat. The mood of foreboding thrusts forward into v. 19: "The scribes and the chief priests tried to lay hands on him at that very hour." Thus Luke has managed to replace the anticipation of Easter with a more historical note, in keeping with his interests in the time sequence of salvation history.

Since we are so obviously confronted with early Christian allegory in this parable, the question about its relationship to Jesus' own teaching cannot be avoided. Even though it is no longer necessary to presuppose that Jesus never, under any circumstances, made allegorical remarks (a simplistic canon of scholarship in the recent past, which ignored an essential strand of prophetic tradition), it remains true that the literary genre of the parable differs essentially from that of allegory. Was this originally an authentic parable?

We cannot know with certainty, but our understanding of this "parable of the wicked tenants" has been greatly enhanced by study of the gnostic Gospel of Thomas and by John Dominic Crossan's analysis of this pericope based on comparison of Thomas's version with the one in the synoptic tradition. The one in Thomas 93:1–18, which Crossan cites, appears to be far more primitive, and independent of the synoptics. The absentee landlord sends just two servants before sending his son, whom the tenants recognize, seize, and kill. The story is capped with the saying, "Whoever has ears let him hear."

Crossan suggests (*In Parables* [New York: Harper & Row, Publishers, 1973]) that what we are to hear is "a deliberately shocking story of successful murder," one which was far from unlikely in the turbulent Galilee of Jesus' day. At its earliest level it was thus neither an allegory nor a moral tale, but a parable of action akin to some of the other master-servant parables which Jesus told. It was a call to a "crisis of reckoning" and to "action in response to the kingdom's advent."

HOMILETICAL INTERPRETATION

There are no immediately obvious relationships and connections among the three texts assigned for this day. The First Lesson is a lucid and unambiguous announcement of the gracious God's new act to deliver his people from the Babylonian exile. The Second Lesson is a central Pauline theme of the two types of righteousness, the one based on the works of the law and the other rooted in God's gracious actions in the death and resurrection of Jesus. The Gospel, the parable of the wicked tenants, is an unconditional announcement of judgment upon the people of God. The judgment falls because the stewards of the Lord's vineyard have failed to accept God's Son as he comes into their midst bringing the kingdom of God with its gift of new life and possibility. The First Lesson and the Gospel might be used antiphonally in a sermon to point to the fast-approaching celebration of the death of Jesus on the cross and his being raised from the dead by God. The good news of the First Lesson and the judgment of the Gospel encompass the totality of the death and resurrection event—the "new thing" God is doing for all people.

First Lesson: Isa. 43:16-21. Exile is a reality of our world. Around the earth are thousands of people who are forced to live behind walls and fences in strange lands because of the power of tyranny or the loss of war. Many other persons are exiled in foreign lands because of revolution or change of political leadership. Yet exile is not only for those whose life has been physically uprooted from their homeland. Many urban apartments, suburban homes, and small-town, rural domiciles house exiles. There are people who are alienated from themselves, their families, their communities, and their God. Exile is not just a physical reality but also a psychological and spiritual reality. The preacher's task is not to dwell overlong on the conditions of Israel's Babylonian exile but to help people see the exiles of our own time, those trapped in the present day by their past or held fast by circumstances over which they have no control. Skin color, economic position, meaninglessness, drug and alcohol dependency are all factors that produce exiles in our communities. The sermon should help the people see the exilic conditions of their own lives.

The word of the Lord to exiles is a surprising and freeing word of promise. The whole of chap. 43 of Isaiah is a magnificent poem of the presence of Yahweh with his people in their trapped situation and the promise that he is going to do a new thing for them. He is going to deliver them and bring them home. Our text recalls the past action of God to deliver his people from their former Egyptian bondage. The people are to remember God's freeing love. But then the Lord tells them to forget that former deliverance, because the new thing he is doing will be beyond comparison and they will perceive it. This new thing is to bring his people back home by the shortest, most direct route through the desert. Not only will God deliver them, but he will also sustain them on their journey by providing water to drink.

The very difficult task for the preacher is to make the word of deliverance as imaginatively powerful and concrete as the word which describes the exile state of the people. The sensitivity of the preacher to the working of God today in the structures and people of the society and the church to heal broken relationships and broken lives can be helpful. Of course, one wants to refer to the new thing that God has done in the death and resurrection of Jesus. God's freeing love made available in that event continues to have power and presence in the lives of people and the world. The Johannine Jesus is described as the way, the truth, and the life, that lead home to the Father. He is also the living water that quenches the parched lives of exiles.

There is yet one other word in the text. The continuing action of God in the lives and world of his chosen people to deliver and restore them has a purpose. The restored people of God are to declare his praise. One of the tasks of ministry of the freed exiles is to sing new songs of praise declaring God's faithful and recreative love. Such doxologies may be heard in the quality of life of the people of God as they live in loving service, being instruments and channels of God's freeing and healing for other exiles.

Second Lesson: Phil. 3:8-14. Strong tensions permeate this text. There is a tension between God's action in Christ and the straining and working that Paul still feels he must do. There is the eschatological tension of the now but not yet that flows from Paul's proclamation of the resurrection. The reality of the power of Christ's resurrection assures life here and now, but it is also not yet finally and fully realized. Paul sees his own life as still sharing in the sufferings and death of Jesus so that he may attain the resurrection from the dead. This tension characterizes the life of the Christian.

The tension, however, does not need to immobilize the believer. God's righteousness revealed through Christ creates hope for the believer. This hope becomes the energizing power for the living of the Christian life. God's love in Christ assures and guarantees the future of the believer with God. No longer do God's people need to spend time and energy being anxious or fearful about the future (see Luke 12:22–34). Now they may spend themselves and their resources in sharing in the sufferings and death of Christ for the sake of the neighbor. "The coming lordship of the risen Christ cannot be merely hoped for and awaited. This hope and expectation also sets its stamp on life, action, and suffering in the history of society. Hence mission means not merely propagation of faith and hope, but also historic transformation of life. The life of the body, including also social and public life, is expected as a sacrifice in day-to-day obedience" (Jürgen Moltmann, *Theology of Hope* [New York: Harper & Row, Publishers, 1967], pp. 329–30).

The sermon arising from this text could speak to the congregation as a community concerning the tensions of this eschatological life given to them in the death and resurrection of Jesus. The sermon could make a clear and concrete announcement of what God has done in order to bring the congregation into relationship with himself and thus to assure their future with him. The particular circumstances of the congregation should be mirrored in this announcement. What are the concrete experiences and expressions of this gracious act of God in their lives? Flowing from this announcement of the manifestation of God's righteousness, the sermon can then help the people discover and see their tasks as people filled with hope. How may they now share in the fellowship of the sufferings of Christ and become like him in his death? What are the concrete situations in the life and ministry of your people that provide the opportunity for them to spend themselves in loving and caring service?

Gospel: Luke 20:9–19. Our Lenten journey is almost complete. We are almost at the beginning point of Holy Week. The gory hill is in view, and the death of Jesus in all of its horror will become centrally fixed in our liturgical experience. One crucial part of the church's understanding of the cross is God's judgment upon all human sin and faithlessness. The judgment note is sounded clearly and frightfully in the Gospel story of the parable of the wicked tenants. For Luke there is no hint of Easter or relaxation of the judgment motif. It is a tale of unmitigated disaster. The religious leaders and the people of Israel have failed the test. They have rejected Jesus and his message of the inbreaking of the kingdom of God. In fact, from the perspective of Luke's story, they even now are trying to devise ways and means to kill him. In the very act of murdering Jesus, Luke says, the leaders and people of Israel bring judgment upon themselves. The stone which they reject will be hurled against them to crush and break them in the divine judgment.

The danger in preaching this parable today is that far too often the preacher finds the enemies of Jesus and God outside the church. Often atheists, Communists, people of other religions become the preacher's targets. Yet the word of judgment in the parable is pronounced upon the church itself. As Pogo says, "We has met the enemy and they is us." This word is a radical challenge to the stewardship that we have performed within the Lord's vineyard of the new Israel. How faithful have we been to the mission entrusted to us? How have we cared for questions of balancing maintenance of the church and ministry to the world? How often have we let the questions of power, glory, and prestige blind us to the way of the cross and suffering on behalf of other people? How has our stubbornness and resistance to change of any kind hindered the free flow of God's creative and redemptive love through our lives and our congregation? How often have we rejected the Lord in our rejection of people who do not measure up to our standards of acceptability and life-style?

The preacher will struggle with ways to put the searching question about the fate of the Son of God as he comes among his people in the church today. The freedom that we enjoy as freed and redeemed sons and daughters of God within the church does not guarantee that we shall not lose our place in the Lord's vineyard. When and if God's people base their lives upon privilege rather than upon responsibility, then God may just raise up new peoples and communities to become the channels of his life-giving grace. Already God has grafted a new branch onto the vine of Israel. Who is to say that he cannot graft another branch onto that vine and prune away the unfruitful and disobedient church?